MATH
INSTANT ASSESSMENTS
for Data Tracking
Grade 2

Visit *carsondellosa.com* for correlations to Common Core, state, national, and Canadian provincial standards.

Carson-Dellosa Publishing, LLC
PO Box 35665
Greensboro, NC 27425 USA
carsondellosa.com

978-1-4838-3611-9
01-339161151

 Table of Contents

✦ Assessment and Data Tracking ✦

Data tracking is an essential element in modern classrooms. Teachers are often required to capture student learning through both formative and summative assessments. They then must use the results to guide teaching, remediation, and lesson planning and provide feedback to students, parents, and administrators. Because time is always at a premium in the classroom, it is vital that teachers have the assessments they need at their fingertips. The assessments need to be suited to the skill being assessed as well as adapted to the stage in the learning process. This is true for an informal checkup at the end of a lesson or a formal assessment at the end of a unit.

This book will provide the tools and assessments needed to determine your students' level of mastery throughout the school year. The assessments are both formal and informal and include a variety of formats—pretests and posttests, flash cards, prompt cards, traditional tests, and exit tickets. Often, there are several assessment options for a single skill or concept to allow you the greatest flexibility when assessing understanding. Simply select the assessment that best fits your needs, or use them all to create a comprehensive set of assessments for before, during, and after learning.

Incorporate Instant Assessments into your daily plans to streamline the data-tracking process and keep the focus on student mastery and growth.

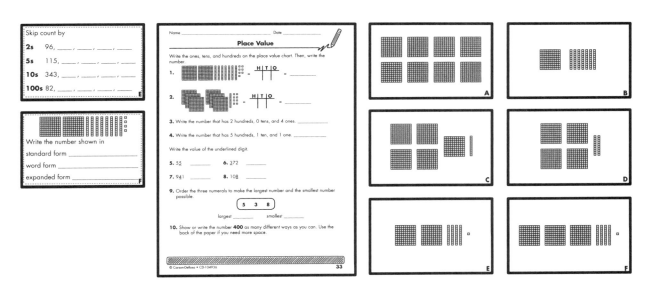

A variety of instant assessments for place value

Types of Assessment

Assessment usually has a negative association because it brings to mind tedious pencil-and-paper tests and grading. However, it can take on many different forms and be a positive, integral part of the year. Not all assessments need to be formal, nor do they all need to be graded. Choose the type of assessment to use based on the information you need to gather. Then, you can decide if or how it should be graded.

	What Does It Look Like?	**Examples**
Formative Assessment	• occurs during learning • is administered frequently • is usually informal and not graded • identifies areas of improvement • provides immediate feedback so a student can make adjustments promptly, if needed • allows teachers to rethink strategies, lesson content, etc., based on current student performance • is process-focused • has the most impact on a student's performance	• in-class observations • exit tickets • reflections and journaling • homework • student-teacher conferences • student self-evaluations
Interim Assessment	• occurs occasionally • is more formal and usually graded • feedback is not immediate, though still fairly quick • helps teachers identify gaps in teaching and areas for remediation • often includes performance assessments, which are individualized, authentic, and performance-based in order to evaluate higher-level thinking skills	• in-class observations • exit tickets • reflections and journaling • homework • student-teacher conferences • student self-evaluations
Summative Assessment	• occurs once learning is considered complete • the information is used by the teacher and school for broader purposes • takes time to return a grade or score • can be used to compare a student's performance to others • is product-focused • has the least impact on a student's performance since there are few or no opportunities for retesting	• cumulative projects • final portfolios • quarterly testing • end-of-the-year testing • standardized testing

The assessments in this book follow a few different formats, depending on the skill or concept being assessed. Use the descriptions below to familiarize yourself with each unique format and get the most out of Instant Assessments all year long.

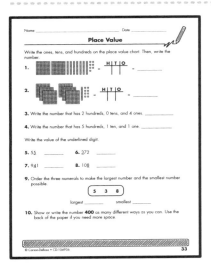

Show What You Know

Each domain begins with a pair of *Show What You Know* tests. Both tests follow the same format and include the same types of questions so they can be directly compared to show growth. Use them as a pretest and posttest. Or, use one as a test at the end of a unit and use the second version as a retest for students after remediation.

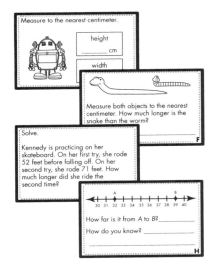

Exit Tickets

Each domain ends with exit tickets that cover the variety of concepts within the domain. Exit tickets are very targeted questions designed to assess understanding of specific skills, so they are ideal formative assessments to use at the end of a lesson. Exit tickets do not have space for student names, allowing teachers to gather information on the entire class without placing pressure on individual students. If desired, have students write their names or initials on the backs of the tickets. Other uses for exit tickets include the following:

- Use the back of each ticket for longer answers, fuller explanations, or extension questions. If needed, students can staple them to larger sheets of paper.
- They can also be used for warm-ups or to find out what students know before a lesson.
- Use the generic exit tickets on pages 7 and 8 for any concept you want to assess. Be sure to fill in any blanks before copying.
- Laminate them and place them in a math center as task cards.
- Use them to play Scoot or a similar review game at the end of a unit.
- Choose several to create a targeted assessment for a skill or set of skills.

Cards

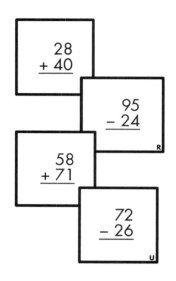

Use the cards as prompts for one-on-one conferencing. Simply copy the cards, cut them apart, and follow the directions preceding each set of cards. Use the lettering to keep track of which cards a student has interacted with.

- Copy on card stock and/or laminate for durability.
- Punch holes in the top left corners and place the cards on a book ring to make them easily accessible.
- Copy the sets on different colors of paper to keep them easily separated or to distinguish different sections within a set of cards.
- Easily differentiate by using different amounts or levels of cards to assess a student.
- Write the answers on the backs of cards to create self-checking flash cards.
- Place them in a math center as task cards or matching activities.
- Use them to play Scoot or a similar review game at the end of a unit.

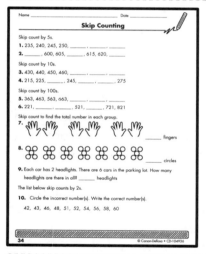

Assessment Pages

The reproducible assessment pages are intended for use as a standard test of a skill. Use them in conjunction with other types of assessment to get a full picture of a student's level of understanding. They can also be used for review or homework.

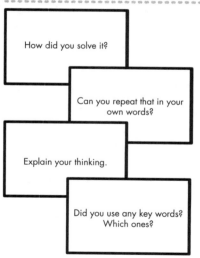

Math Talk Prompt Cards

Use the math talk prompt cards on pages 9 and 10 to prompt math discussions that can be used to informally assess students' levels of understanding. Use the math talk prompts to encourage reflection and deeper understanding of math concepts throughout the year.

- Copy on card stock and/or laminate for durability.
- Punch holes in the top left corners and place the cards on a book ring to keep them easily accessible.
- Use them for journaling prompts.
- Place them in a math center to be used with other activities.

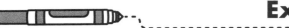

Exit Tickets

Exit tickets are a useful formative assessment tool that you can easily work into your day. You can choose to use a single exit ticket at the end of the day or at the end of each lesson. Simply choose a ticket below, and make one copy for each student. Then, have students complete the prompt and present them to you as their ticket out of the door. Use the student responses to gauge overall learning, create small remediation groups, or target areas for reteaching. A blank exit ticket is included on page 8 so you can create your own exit tickets as well.

What stuck with you today?

_____
_____
_____
_____

List three facts you learned today. Put them in order from most important to least important.

1. _____
2. _____
3. _____

The first thing I'll tell my family about today is

_____
_____
_____
_____

The most important thing I learned today is

_____
_____
_____
_____

Color the face that shows how you feel about understanding today's lesson.

Explain why. _____
_____

Summarize today's lesson in 10 words or less.

_____
_____
_____
_____

One example of _____ is _____

_____

_____ .

One question I still have is _____

_____

_____

_____ .

How will understanding _____

_____

help you in real life? _____

_____

_____

One new word I learned today is

_____ .

It means _____

_____

_____ .

Draw a picture related to the lesson. Add a caption.

_____

_____

If today's lesson were a song, the title would be _____

_____

because _____

_____ .

The answer is _____ .

What is the question? _____

_____

_____

_____

Use these prompts when observing individual students in order to better understand their thinking and depth of understanding of a concept. These cards may also be used during whole-class lessons or in small remediation groups to encourage students to explain their thinking with different concepts.

How did you solve it?	What strategy did you use?
How could you solve it a different way?	Can you repeat that in your own words?
Explain your thinking.	Did you use any key words? Which ones?

Can you explain why you chose to do that?	Why did you choose to add/subtract/ multiply/divide?
How do you know your answer is correct?	How can you prove your answer?
Is this like any other problems you have solved? How?	What would change if . . . ?
Why is _____ important?	What do you need to do next? Why?

✦ Show What You Know ✦
Operations and Algebraic Thinking

1. Write *even* or *odd* to complete the sentence.

There is an _____ amount of cookies.

2. Circle *even* or *odd* for each number.

    24   even   odd

    11   even   odd

    77   even   odd

3. Write an addition sentence to prove that each number is even.

$6 = $ _____ $+$ _____

$14 = $ _____ $+$ _____

$20 = $ _____ $+$ _____

4. How many dots? _____

Write an addition sentence to show your answer.

_____

Solve. Show your work.

5. Sierra is constructing a spaceship out of plastic blocks. On the first day, she completed 14 pages in the instruction booklet. On the second day, she completed 23 pages in the booklet. How many pages has she completed so far?

6. John's dog weighs 37 pounds. His friend Rosa's dog weighs 11 pounds. How much more does John's dog weigh than Rosa's?

7. Rebecca has 15 books. Zane has 13 books. Owen has 20 books. They donated 25 books to the library. How many books do they have left?

8.

9	15	2	18	12
+ 6	− 7	+ 8	− 9	− 9

9.

6	4	7	3	13
− 2	− 4	+ 5	+ 9	− 4

10.

8	11	1	5	17
+ 3	− 9	+ 6	− 1	− 9

11.

2	5	12	5	8
+ 3	+ 5	− 4	+ 3	− 8

12.

10	7	14	3	10
− 8	+ 3	− 6	+ 4	− 5

Name _____   Date _____

✦ Show What You Know ✦
Operations and Algebraic Thinking

1. Write *even* or *odd* to complete the sentence.

There is an _____ amount of hats.

2. Circle *even* or *odd* for each number.

16   even   odd

63   even   odd

50   even   odd

3. Write an addition sentence to prove that each number is even.

8 = _____ + _____

16 = _____ + _____

12 = _____ + _____

4. How many dots? _____

Write an addition sentence to show your answer.

_____

Solve. Show your work.

5. At the park, there are 57 elm trees. There are 42 maple trees. How many elm and maple trees are there in the park altogether?

6. The farmer has 75 rows of corn. So far, he has harvested corn from 41 rows. How many rows does he have left to harvest from?

7. Luke read 42 pages in his book last night. Today, he read 46 pages. If there are 100 pages in his book, how many pages does Luke have left to read?

8.

3	15	14	1	5
+ 3	− 8	− 6	+ 9	+ 5

9.

4	4	11	5	17
+ 5	+ 1	− 2	+ 8	− 8

10.

11	6	3	9	2
− 4	+ 7	+ 6	− 6	+ 5

11.

4	5	13	11	5
+ 2	− 4	− 6	− 7	+ 2

12.

8	13	6	12	2
+ 2	− 5	+ 5	− 7	+ 1

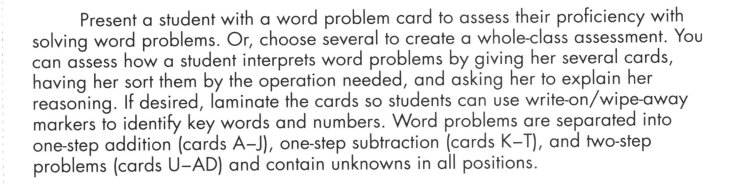

Word Problems

Present a student with a word problem card to assess their proficiency with solving word problems. Or, choose several to create a whole-class assessment. You can assess how a student interprets word problems by giving her several cards, having her sort them by the operation needed, and asking her to explain her reasoning. If desired, laminate the cards so students can use write-on/wipe-away markers to identify key words and numbers. Word problems are separated into one-step addition (cards A–J), one-step subtraction (cards K–T), and two-step problems (cards U–AD) and contain unknowns in all positions.

Near Victor's house, 7 grocery stores and 16 gas stations are open daily. How many grocery stores and gas stations are there near Victor's house? **A**	Sam's Sporting Goods Store has 15 baseball bats. It also has 18 baseball gloves. How many bats and gloves does Sam's Sporting Goods Store have in all? **B**
Mrs. Gladd's class has 22 desks. Mr. Walsh's class has 25 desks. How many desks do Mrs. Gladd and Mr. Walsh have in all? **C**	Lamar counted 60 fans sitting in the bleachers. Mia counted 13 more fans standing. How many fans are in the bleachers in all? **D**
Neil practiced piano for 54 minutes Saturday morning. Later that day, he practiced for 22 more minutes. How many minutes did he practice in all? **E**	Twenty-eight beads were in a bowl. Tisha added seventy-seven more beads. How many beads does Tisha have now? **F**

Anton buys 61 peaches at the farmers market. Bonnie picks 27 peaches at the peach orchard. How many peaches do Anton and Bonnie have altogether?

G

On Monday, 53 students were in the library in the morning. That afternoon, 29 more students came to check out books. How many students visited the library on Monday?

H

Kelsey put 8 skirts, 25 pairs of pants, and 28 shirts in her closet. How many items of clothing did Kelsey put away?

I

The bakery sold 12 cupcakes on Monday, 24 cupcakes on Tuesday, 18 cupcakes on Wednesday, and 33 cupcakes on Thursday. How many cupcakes has the bakery sold so far this week?

J

Zoe and Jill made 17 friendship bracelets. Zoe made 8 of the bracelets. How many friendship bracelets did Jill make?

K

There are twenty swings at the park. Sixteen of the swings are empty. How many swings are being used?

L

Mr. Upton bought 24 cupcakes for Robert's birthday. After the party, there were 8 cupcakes left. How many cupcakes were eaten at the party?

M

Avery bought twenty-six tomatoes at the farmers' market. Fourteen of them were grape tomatoes and the rest were cherry tomatoes. How many cherry tomatoes did Avery buy?

N

Before Mrs. Ramirez's class came to lunch, there were 36 slices of pizza. After they were finished, there were 19 slices left. How many slices of pizza did Mrs. Ramirez's class eat?

O

Grace had 45 stamps when she left for camp. While at camp, she writes 21 letters. She uses one stamp on each letter. How many stamps does Grace have left?

P

Gavin has 59 blocks in a bag. If 34 of the blocks are cubes and the rest are rectangular prisms, how many of the blocks are rectangular prisms?

Q

Leslie has 60 minutes to play outside. She rode her bike for 27 minutes. How much time does she have left outside?

R

Ross counts 73 animals at the pet store. He counts 27 lizards in the reptile section and some fish in the fish tanks. How many fish did he count in the fish tanks?

S

Quan borrowed a library book with 96 pages. He has read 37 pages so far. How many pages does he have left in the book?

T

Amira gathered 13 eggs in the morning. She gathered 9 more in the evening. She dropped 7 and broke them. How many eggs does she have left?

U

Nassim collects action figures. He already has 28 in his collection. He bought 6 more. Then, he gave his little brother 3 to keep. How many action figures does he have left?

V

At the carnival, Shelby scooped 26 scoops of ice cream. Rudy scooped 10 more scoops than Shelby. How many scoops of ice cream did they scoop in all?

W

Kyle rode his bike for 40 minutes on Saturday. He rode his bike for 15 less minutes on Sunday. How much time did he spend riding his bike all weekend?

X

Mrs. Ling's class is reading a 100-page book. Last week they read 56 pages. This week they read 38 pages. How many pages do they have left to read in the book?

Y

Nora got $100 on her birthday. She spent $12 on a new doll and $31 on outfits for the doll. How much money does she have left?

Z

Ian was weighing his three guinea pigs. Chocolate weighs 28 ounces. Speedy weighs 31 ounces. When he put all three of them on the scale, it showed 95 ounces. How much does his other guinea pig, Fritz, weigh?

AA

Liza helped her mom in the garden. She picked 14 peppers, 9 squash, and 8 zucchini. They used 6 of the vegetables she picked to make dinner. How many vegetables are left?

AB

Apples are 10 cents each at the farmers' market. James chose 4 green apples and 2 red apples. How much did he spend on apples?

AC

Olivia brought 48 crayons and 30 markers to her friend's house. When she got home, she had 73 crayons and markers in all. Did she lose any? If so, how many?

AD

Even and Odd Sets

Use these cards to assess a student's proficiency with even and odd sets. You may choose to give a student the whole set and have him sort them into even sets and odd sets or show one card at a time and have the student tell if it shows an even or odd number. If desired, laminate the cards to allow students to use write-on/wipe-away markers and draw on the sets.

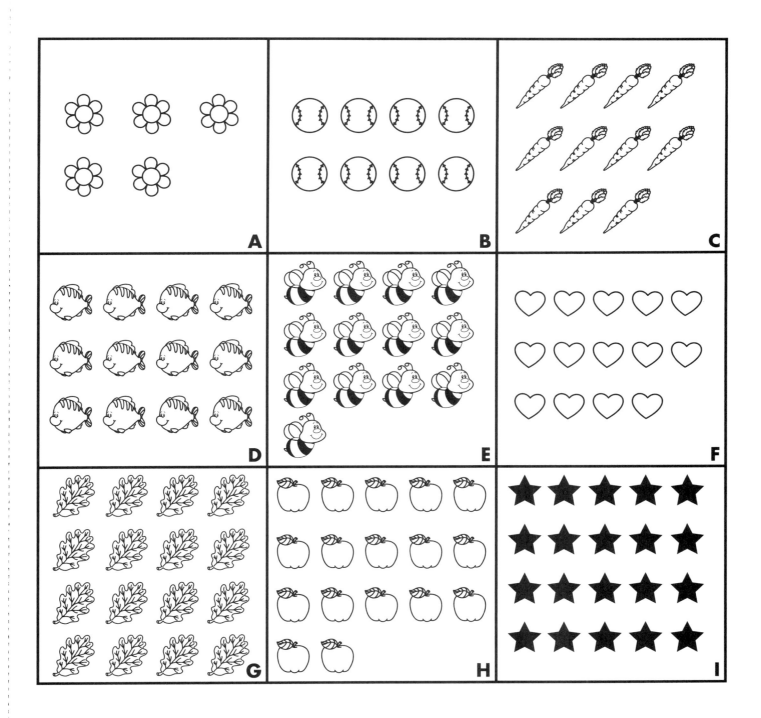

Even and Odd Numbers

1. Color the even numbers orange. Color the odd numbers blue.

1	2	3	4	5	6	7	8	9	10
11	12	13	14	15	16	17	18	19	20

2. Explain how you can tell if a number is odd or even.

_____

_____

3. Sort the numbers using the chart.

23	31
37	40
49	52
68	74
85	96

Even	**Odd**

Write an addition sentence to prove that each number is even.

4.   8 = _____ + _____

5.   14 = _____ + _____

6.   12 = _____ + _____

7.   4 = _____ + _____

8.   10 = _____ + _____

9.   6 = _____ + _____

10. Write an odd number. _____

Write an even number. _____

Arrays

Use these cards to assess a student's proficiency in understanding arrays and repeated addition sentences. Provide the student with a card or set of cards. Have him write the repeated addition sentence shown by the array. If desired, laminate the cards so students can use write-on/wipe-away markers to write the repeated addition sentences on the cards or circle each row or column. Cards can be turned vertically or horizontally to show related arrays. Use the blank card to replace a lost card or to add another array of your choosing to the set.

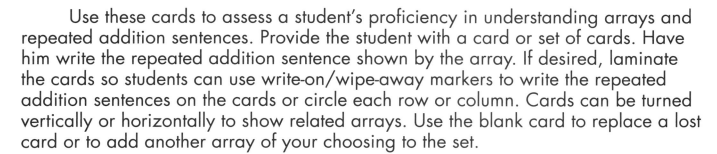

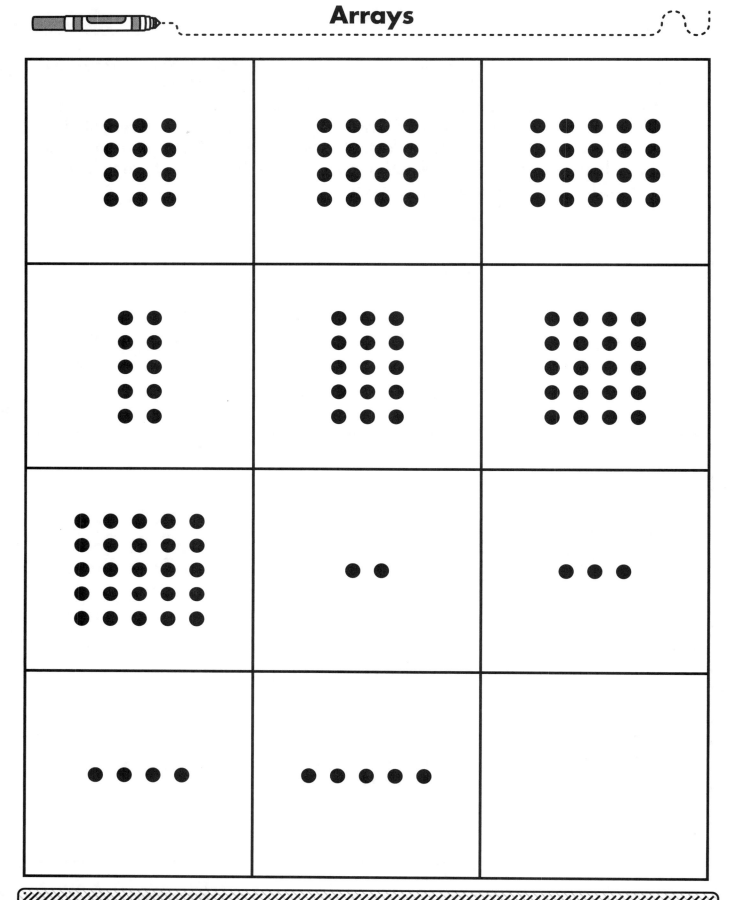

Arrays

Look at each array. Write the repeated addition sentence.

1. ⬜⬜⬜⬜
⬜⬜⬜⬜
⬜⬜⬜⬜
⬜⬜⬜⬜

_____ = _____

2. ○○○○○
○○○○○

_____ = _____

3. △△△△△
△△△△△
△△△△△

_____ = _____

4. ☆☆☆☆
☆☆☆☆

_____ = _____

5. ○○○○○
○○○○○
○○○○○
○○○○○

_____ = _____

6. △△△
△△△
△△△
△△△

_____ = _____

7. ⬡⬡⬡
⬡⬡⬡

_____ = _____

8. ☽☽☽
☽☽☽
☽☽☽

_____ = _____

Draw an array to match each addition sentence. Then, solve.

9. 4 + 4 + 4 = _____

10. 5 + 5 = _____

Fact Fluency within 20

Solve.

1.
$$2 + 6$$
$$14 - 8$$
$$9 - 2$$
$$6 + 5$$
$$2 + 3$$

2.
$$12 - 6$$
$$3 + 9$$
$$4 + 7$$
$$12 - 5$$
$$7 - 3$$

3.
$$8 + 4$$
$$6 - 3$$
$$3 + 4$$
$$8 + 1$$
$$11 - 4$$

4.
$$3 - 1$$
$$3 + 2$$
$$11 - 7$$
$$8 + 2$$
$$12 - 3$$

5.
$$7 + 5$$
$$10 - 2$$
$$3 + 6$$
$$6 - 1$$
$$9 - 4$$

6.
$$8 + 2$$
$$8 + 9$$
$$13 - 9$$
$$4 + 1$$
$$12 - 7$$

7.
$$10 - 3$$
$$1 + 4$$
$$12 - 6$$
$$8 + 5$$
$$2 + 7$$

8.
$$2 - 2$$
$$7 + 7$$
$$4 + 3$$
$$10 - 7$$
$$11 - 5$$

9.
$$9 - 2$$
$$6 + 9$$
$$17 - 8$$
$$8 + 8$$
$$6 - 3$$

10.
$$3 + 5$$
$$12 - 4$$
$$4 + 1$$
$$15 - 6$$
$$8 + 6$$

Score

| 1 | 2 | 3 | 4 | 5 |

Minutes

A. Abbie fed her rabbit Nibbles 22 green peas. Nibbles left 7 peas in the bowl. How many peas did Nibbles eat?

+ or **−** ?

How do you know? _____

_____

_____

B. Ben had 7 Action Mack figures. After his birthday he had 13 Action Mack figures in all. How many figures did Ben get for his birthday?

Choose the best number sentence to solve this problem.

$7 - ? = 13$ $\qquad$ $7 + ? = 13$

C. Solve.

While hiking, Delia saw 9 robins, 3 bluebirds, and 15 cardinals. How many birds did she see in all?

D. Solve.

The Wildcats scored 16 points in the first half. They scored 21 points in the second half. The other team scored 26 points in all. Did the Wildcats score enough to win? If so, by how many points?

E. Solve.

1. $5 - 3 =$ _____ $\quad$ **2.** $11 - 4 =$ _____

3. $7 + 6 =$ _____ $\quad$ **4.** $8 + 4 =$ _____

5. $9 - 2 =$ _____ $\quad$ **6.** $6 + 9 =$ _____

7. $3 + 11 =$ _____ $\quad$ **8.** $18 - 8 =$ _____

F. Write the number that makes each number sentence true.

1. $5 +$ ____ $= 11$ $\quad$ **2.** ____ $+ 9 = 14$

3. $4 +$ ____ $= 12$ $\quad$ **4.** $8 -$ ____ $= 2$

5. ____ $- 7 = 8$ $\quad$ **6.** ____ $+ 2 = 11$

7. $16 -$ ____ $= 6$ $\quad$ **8.** ____ $- 3 = 13$

G.
Start with 10.
Add 4.
Subtract 7.
Add 13.

What is your answer?

_____

Start with 15.
Subtract 6.
Subtract 8.
Add 10.

What is your answer?

_____

H.
Start with 20.
Subtract 12.
Subtract 3.
Add 10.

What is your answer?

_____

Start with 10.
Double it.
Add 7.
Subtract 9.

What is your answer?

_____

I.

• • • • • • •	★ ★ ★ ★ ★	▲ ▲ ▲ ▲ ▲ ▲
• • • • • • •	★ ★ ★ ★ ★	▲ ▲ ▲ ▲ ▲ ▲
• • • • •		▲ ▲
even	even	even
odd	odd	odd

J.

Tell if each number is **even** or **odd**.

1. 16 _____   **2.** 47 _____

3. 99 _____   **4.** 32 _____

5. 28 _____   **6.** 80 _____

7. 55 _____   **8.** 71 _____

K.

Write an addition sentence for each even set.

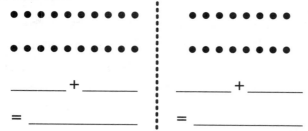

_____ + _____   _____ + _____

= _____   = _____

L.

Without adding, circle the equations with even sums. Draw a box around the equations with odd sums.

$3 + 9$ $1 + 4$ $8 + 5$

$2 + 6$ $7 + 6$ $6 + 10$

M.

How many? _____

N.

• • •
• • • $2 + 3$

Is the number sentence correct?

yes   no

Why or why not? _____

_____

O.

Write an addition sentence for the array.

_____

_____

P.

$3 + 3 + 3 + 3 + 3$

Draw the array for this number sentence.

✦ Show What You Know ✦
Number and Operations in Base Ten

1. What number is represented?

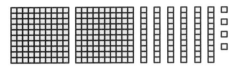

_____

2. Write the value of the underlined digit.

109 _____

882 _____

360 _____

3. Use **<**, **>**, or **=** to compare.

205 ◯ 145

887 ◯ 978

560 ◯ 562

4. Place the numbers in order from least to greatest.

345   354   432   234

_____, _____, _____, _____

5. Write 704 in expanded form.

_____

Then, write it in word form.

_____

_____

6. Write 459 in expanded form.

_____

Then, write it in word form.

_____

_____

7. Use skip counting to fill in the missing numbers.

By 5s

125, _____, _____, 140, 145

By 10s

68, 78, _____, 98, _____

By 100s

317, _____, 517, 617, _____

8. Use skip counting to solve.

Five lemons come in a bag. Ben bought six bags of lemons to use for his lemonade stand. How many lemons did Ben buy?

Add.

9. $\begin{array}{r} 67 \\ +\ 31 \\ \hline \end{array}$ **10.** $\begin{array}{r} 35 \\ +\ 23 \\ \hline \end{array}$ **11.** $\begin{array}{r} 57 \\ +\ 39 \\ \hline \end{array}$ **12.** $\begin{array}{r} 88 \\ +\ 13 \\ \hline \end{array}$

13. $\begin{array}{r} 462 \\ +\ 107 \\ \hline \end{array}$ **14.** $\begin{array}{r} 620 \\ +\ 153 \\ \hline \end{array}$ **15.** $\begin{array}{r} 519 \\ +\ 264 \\ \hline \end{array}$ **16.** $\begin{array}{r} 908 \\ +\ 174 \\ \hline \end{array}$

Subtract.

17. $\begin{array}{r} 75 \\ -\ 44 \\ \hline \end{array}$ **18.** $\begin{array}{r} 56 \\ -\ 13 \\ \hline \end{array}$ **19.** $\begin{array}{r} 61 \\ -\ 24 \\ \hline \end{array}$ **20.** $\begin{array}{r} 80 \\ -\ 52 \\ \hline \end{array}$

21. $\begin{array}{r} 552 \\ -\ 140 \\ \hline \end{array}$ **22.** $\begin{array}{r} 675 \\ -\ 343 \\ \hline \end{array}$ **23.** $\begin{array}{r} 424 \\ -\ 268 \\ \hline \end{array}$ **24.** $\begin{array}{r} 617 \\ -\ 557 \\ \hline \end{array}$

Solve each problem in your head. Record the answer.

25. $539 + 10 =$ _____ **26.** $226 - 10 =$ _____

27. $821 + 100 =$ _____ **28.** $385 - 100 =$ _____

✦ Show What You Know ✦
Number and Operations in Base Ten

1. What number is represented?

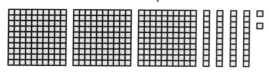

_____

2. Write the value of the underlined digit.

90<u>3</u> _____

<u>2</u>81 _____

6<u>4</u>7 _____

3. Use **<**, **>**, or **=** to compare.

515 ◯ 551

206 ◯ 236

140 ◯ 405

4. Place the numbers in order from least to greatest.

552   520   251   220

_____ , _____ , _____ , _____

5. Write 643 in expanded form.

_____

Then, write it in word form.

_____

_____

6. Write 805 in expanded form.

_____

Then, write it in word form.

_____

_____

7. Use skip counting to fill in the missing numbers.

By 5s

565, _____ , 575, _____ , 585

By 10s

112, 122, _____ , _____ , 152

By 100s

574, _____ , 774, 874, _____

8. Use skip counting to solve.

There are 10 people in each row of the parade. There are 7 rows in all. How many people are marching in the parade?

Add.

9. 43
    + 24

10. 61
     + 36

11. 46
     + 27

12. 77
     + 44

13. 704
     + 154

14. 468
     + 311

15. 402
     + 359

16. 566
     + 474

Subtract.

17. 97
     − 43

18. 82
     − 31

19. 40
     − 29

20. 73
     − 56

21. 748
     − 512

22. 593
     − 470

23. 415
     − 226

24. 803
     − 545

Solve each problem in your head. Record the answer.

25. 316 + 10 = _____

26. 592 − 10 = _____

27. 660 + 100 = _____

28. 473 − 100 = _____

Base Ten Models

Use these cards to assess students' understanding of place value concepts. Present a student with a card or cards and have her give the value or have her tell the number of ones, tens, or hundreds in the model. You may also choose to have her write the number in standard form, word form, and/or expanded form.

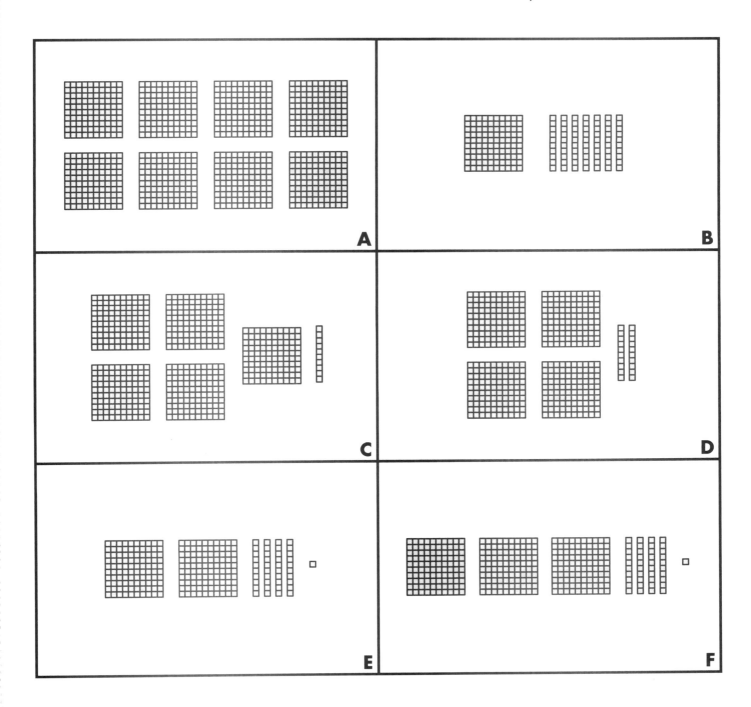

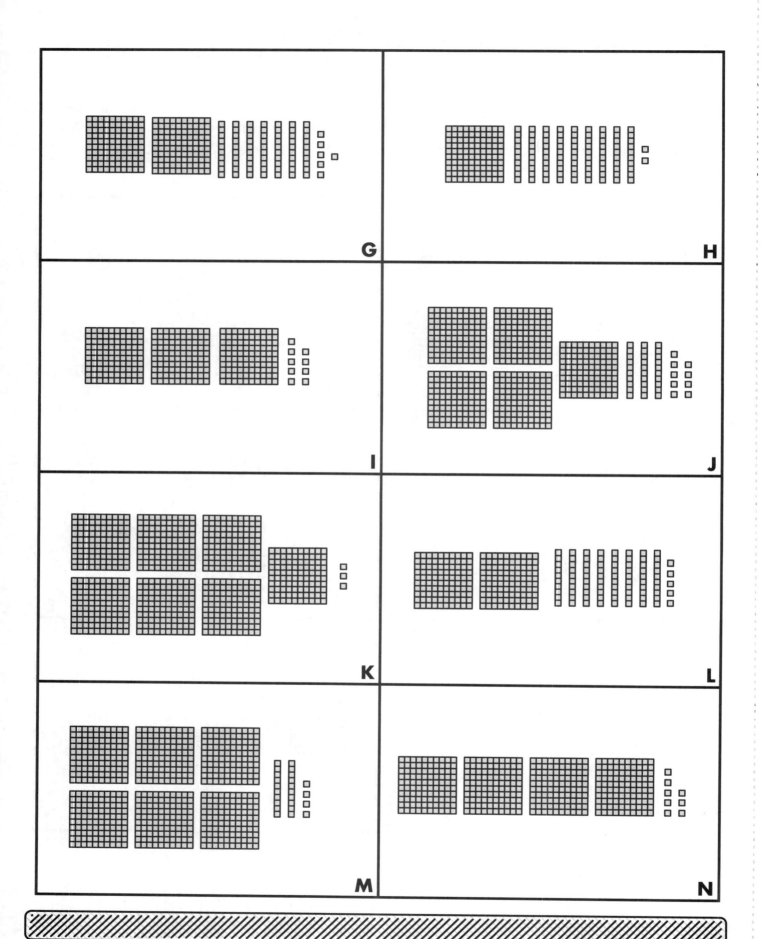

Place Value

Write the ones, tens, and hundreds on the place value chart. Then, write the number.

1. 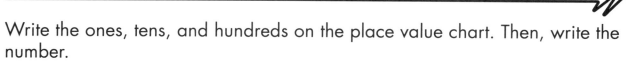 = H | T | O = _____

2. 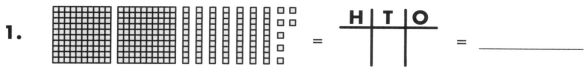 = H | T | O = _____

3. Write the number that has 2 hundreds, 0 tens, and 4 ones. _____

4. Write the number that has 5 hundreds, 1 ten, and 1 one. _____

Write the value of the underlined digit.

5. 5<u>5</u> _____   **6.** <u>3</u>72 _____

7. 9<u>4</u>1 _____   **8.** 10<u>8</u> _____

9. Order the three numerals to make the largest number and the smallest number possible.

> 5   3   8

largest _____   smallest _____

10. Show or write the number **400** as many different ways as you can. Use the back of the paper if you need more space.

Skip Counting

Skip count by 5s.

1. 235, 240, 245, 250, _____ , _____ , _____

2. _____ , 600, 605, _____ , 615, 620, _____

Skip count by 10s.

3. 430, 440, 450, 460, _____ , _____ , _____

4. 215, 225, _____ , 245, _____ , _____ , 275

Skip count by 100s.

5. 363, 463, 563, 663, _____ , _____ , _____

6. 221, _____ , _____ , 521, _____ , 721, 821

Skip count to find the total number in each group.

7.

_____ fingers

8.

_____ circles

9. Each car has 2 headlights. There are 6 cars in the parking lot. How many

headlights are there in all? _____ headlights

10. The list skip counts by 2s. Circle each incorrect number. Then, write the
correct number below each circle.

42, 43, 46, 48, 51, 52, 54, 56, 58, 60

Number Forms

Look at the place value blocks. Write the standard, expanded, and word forms of each number.

1.

Standard form: _____   Expanded form: _____

Word form: _____

2.

Standard form: _____   Expanded form: _____

Word form: _____

Write the matching number.

3. 700 + 10 + 4 _____   **4.** 200 + 60 + 7 _____

5. nine hundred ten _____   **6.** 400 + 70 + 8 _____

7. eight hundred twelve _____   **8.** one hundred ninety-five _____

Write each number in expanded form.

9. seven hundred thirty-four   **10.** 601

_____   _____

Write each number in word form.

11. 900 + 70 + 5

_____

12. 800 + 30

_____

Comparing Numbers

Use **<**, **>**, or **=** to compare.

1. 117 ◯ 107

2. 507 ◯ 862

3. 268 ◯ 268

4. 645 ◯ 654

5. 713 ◯ 476

6. 16 ◯ 164

Circle the number in each set that is greatest.

7. 36   52   49

8.   629   727   726

9. 274   261   217

10. 868   888   880

11. 145   194   149

12. 232   334   221   144   322

Write each set of numbers in order from least to greatest.

13. 121, 111, 131, 91 _____

14. 623, 632, 601, 610 _____

15. Explain how you know that 540 is greater than 440.

_____

_____

Identifying Regrouping

Use these cards to determine whether a student understands when regrouping is needed or as a quick addition or subtraction assessment. Provide the student with several cards to sort according to whether or not the problem shown needs regrouping to solve it. Or, use the cards as prompt cards for students to solve. If desired, use only the addition cards (A–J) or only the subtraction cards (K–U).

28 + 40 **A**	58 + 32 **B**	62 + 35 **C**
53 + 16 **D**	65 + 28 **E**	73 + 14 **F**
58 + 71 **G**	44 + 76 **H**	47 + 41 **I**

$\begin{array}{r} 27 \\ + 14 \\ \hline \end{array}$	$\begin{array}{r} 90 \\ - 31 \\ \hline \end{array}$	$\begin{array}{r} 96 \\ - 22 \\ \hline \end{array}$
J	K	L
$\begin{array}{r} 58 \\ - 39 \\ \hline \end{array}$	$\begin{array}{r} 64 \\ - 17 \\ \hline \end{array}$	$\begin{array}{r} 47 \\ - 27 \\ \hline \end{array}$
M	N	O
$\begin{array}{r} 32 \\ - 11 \\ \hline \end{array}$	$\begin{array}{r} 85 \\ - 47 \\ \hline \end{array}$	$\begin{array}{r} 95 \\ - 24 \\ \hline \end{array}$
P	Q	R
$\begin{array}{r} 43 \\ - 25 \\ \hline \end{array}$	$\begin{array}{r} 38 \\ - 16 \\ \hline \end{array}$	$\begin{array}{r} 72 \\ - 26 \\ \hline \end{array}$
S	T	U

Adding Two-Digit Numbers within 100 without Regrouping

Solve.

1. 27 + 62	**2.** 95 + 4	**3.** 42 + 6	**4.** 75 + 12
5. 62 + 6	**6.** 61 + 30	**7.** 56 + 12	**8.** 73 + 26
9. 46 + 51	**10.** 33 + 42	**11.** 50 + 29	**12.** 64 + 25
13. 32 + 62	**14.** 53 + 32	**15.** 49 + 40	**16.** 83 + 14
17. 75 + 23	**18.** 45 + 11	**19.** 46 + 41	**20.** 84 + 15

Adding Two-Digit Numbers within 100 with Regrouping

Solve.

1. 56
    + 6

2. 38
    + 3

3. 85
    + 15

4. 36
    + 25

5. 77
    + 5

6. 55
    + 26

7. 72
    + 29

8. 58
    + 13

9. 65
    + 27

10. 81
    + 19

11. 24
    + 19

12. 94
    + 26

13. 37
    + 36

14. 84
    + 27

15. 75
    + 47

16. 68
    + 24

17. 28
    + 26

18. 49
    + 18

19. 54
    + 27

20. 39
    + 22

Adding More Than Two
Two-Digit Numbers

Solve.

1.
```
  36
  12
+ 25
```
73

2.
```
  48
  32
+ 26
```
106

3.
```
  72
  54
+ 13
```
139

4. 37 + 99 + 34 = 170

```
  37
  99
+ 34
─────
 170
```

5. 28 + 19 + 65 = 112

```
  28
  19
+ 65
─────
```

6.
```
  29
  51
  15
+ 30
```
125

7.
```
  12
  64
  22
+ 36
```
134

8.
```
  15
  43
  72
+ 21
```
151

9. 47 + 28 + 11 + 31 = 117

```
  47
  28
  11
+ 31
```

10. 39 + 70 + 18 + 42 = 169

Name _____ Date _____

Subtracting Two-Digit Numbers within 100 without Regrouping

Solve.

1. 77 − 5	**2.** 95 − 21	**3.** 56 − 14	**4.** 68 − 6
5. 43 − 11	**6.** 67 − 23	**7.** 36 − 25	**8.** 83 − 30
9. 72 − 51	**10.** 43 − 3	**11.** 27 − 13	**12.** 58 − 24
13. 75 − 34	**14.** 52 − 21	**15.** 82 − 61	**16.** 75 − 31
17. 74 − 40	**18.** 37 − 12	**19.** 39 − 27	**20.** 49 − 32

Subtracting Two-Digit Numbers within 100 with Regrouping

Solve.

1.   35
      – 7

2.   26
      – 18

3.   48
      – 9

4.   21
      – 14

5.   57
      – 38

6.   33
      – 26

7.   70
      – 56

8.   82
      – 13

9.   62
      – 47

10.   55
       – 39

11.   91
       – 23

12.   44
       – 29

13.   94
       – 56

14.   85
       – 29

15.   51
       – 38

16.   70
       – 41

17.   42
       – 27

18.   22
       – 19

19.   62
       – 45

20.   80
       – 23

Addition and Subtraction within 100

Solve.

1. $\begin{array}{r} 81 \\ -72 \\ \hline \end{array}$

2. $\begin{array}{r} 35 \\ +14 \\ \hline \end{array}$

3. $\begin{array}{r} 28 \\ +61 \\ \hline \end{array}$

4. $\begin{array}{r} 72 \\ -55 \\ \hline \end{array}$

5. $\begin{array}{r} 51 \\ +39 \\ \hline \end{array}$

6. $\begin{array}{r} 99 \\ -34 \\ \hline \end{array}$

7. $\begin{array}{r} 60 \\ +27 \\ \hline \end{array}$

8. $\begin{array}{r} 51 \\ -37 \\ \hline \end{array}$

9. $\begin{array}{r} 65 \\ -21 \\ \hline \end{array}$

10. $\begin{array}{r} 84 \\ +77 \\ \hline \end{array}$

11. $\begin{array}{r} 47 \\ -19 \\ \hline \end{array}$

12. $\begin{array}{r} 55 \\ +28 \\ \hline \end{array}$

13. $\begin{array}{r} 46 \\ +23 \\ \hline \end{array}$

14. $\begin{array}{r} 63 \\ -29 \\ \hline \end{array}$

15. $\begin{array}{r} 80 \\ -56 \\ \hline \end{array}$

16. $\begin{array}{r} 57 \\ +44 \\ \hline \end{array}$

17. $\begin{array}{r} 78 \\ -34 \\ \hline \end{array}$

18. $\begin{array}{r} 31 \\ -18 \\ \hline \end{array}$

19. $\begin{array}{r} 89 \\ +76 \\ \hline \end{array}$

20. $\begin{array}{r} 37 \\ +28 \\ \hline \end{array}$

Adding Three-Digit Numbers within 1,000 without Regrouping

Solve.

1. 412
   + 313

2. 639
   + 210

3. 257
   + 142

4. 574
   + 324

5. 332
   + 647

6. 281
   + 114

7. 528
   + 161

8. 450
   + 326

9. 261
   + 223

10. 155
    + 142

11. 336
    + 461

12. 506
    + 482

13. 483
    + 211

14. 710
    + 125

15. 243
    + 146

16. 516
    + 471

17. 351
    + 422

18. 818
    + 170

19. 652
    + 236

20. 335
    + 234

Name _____ Date _____

Adding Three-Digit Numbers within 1,000 with Regrouping

Solve.

1. 395 + 425	**2.** 273 + 184	**3.** 572 + 159	**4.** 454 + 168
5. 328 + 543	**6.** 756 + 107	**7.** 325 + 239	**8.** 901 + 149
9. 855 + 416	**10.** 370 + 187	**11.** 926 + 106	**12.** 379 + 219
13. 825 + 427	**14.** 421 + 380	**15.** 532 + 481	**16.** 493 + 177
17. 716 + 235	**18.** 554 + 237	**19.** 629 + 103	**20.** 486 + 216

Subtracting Three-Digit Numbers
within 1,000 without Regrouping

Solve.

1. 548
  − 101

2. 495
  − 360

3. 179
  − 154

4. 262
  − 141

5. 474
  − 213

6. 989
  − 468

7. 537
  − 226

8. 688
  − 253

9. 495
  − 311

10. 757
  − 412

11. 852
  − 510

12. 617
  − 404

13. 367
  − 153

14. 922
  − 602

15. 598
  − 526

16. 289
  − 127

17. 477
  − 234

18. 185
  − 132

19. 719
  − 406

20. 671
  − 340

Name _____   Date _____

Subtracting Three-Digit Numbers within 1,000 with Regrouping

Solve.

1. 261
  − 149

2. 726
  − 237

3. 537
  − 229

4. 612
  − 328

5. 428
  − 183

6. 625
  − 337

7. 852
  − 163

8. 370
  − 258

9. 792
  − 618

10. 900
  − 354

11. 707
  − 522

12. 395
  − 207

13. 851
  − 399

14. 435
  − 136

15. 711
  − 213

16. 921
  − 542

17. 517
  − 172

18. 294
  − 196

19. 381
  − 222

20. 600
  − 413

Addition and Subtraction
within 1,000

Solve.

1.   561
        + 311

2.   489
        + 101

3.   456
        − 213

4.   951
        − 258

5.   592
        + 238

6.   780
        − 450

7.   511
        + 364

8.   332
        − 145

9.   643
        − 407

10.   248
         + 177

11.   588
         − 309

12.   917
         + 166

13.   622
         + 261

14.   429
         − 206

15.   724
         − 555

16.   447
         + 264

17.   853
         − 199

18.   703
         + 289

19.   200
         − 157

20.   361
         + 341

Name _____ Date _____

Adding and Subtracting 10 and 100

Look at each number in the middle column. Write the numbers that are 10 less and 10 more or 100 less and 100 more.

	10 Less	**10 More**		**100 Less**	**100 More**
1.	_____	11 _____	**4.**	_____	491 _____
2.	_____	53 _____	**5.**	_____	662 _____
3.	_____	94 _____	**6.**	_____	808 _____

Solve.

7.	**8.**	**9.**	**10.**	**11.**	**12.**
68 + 10	37 + 10	351 + 10	51 − 10	82 − 10	994 − 10

13.	**14.**	**15.**	**16.**	**17.**	**18.**
71 + 100	285 + 100	873 + 100	650 − 100	472 − 100	121 − 100

19. Explain how to add or subtract 10 from a number.

_____

_____

20. Explain how to add or subtract 100 from a number.

_____

_____

A

Show the number four different ways.

(24)

B

Show the number four different ways.

(315)

C

Write the value of the underlined digit.

9_2_6 _____   _8_14 _____

_3_37 _____   40_9_ _____

Circle the number that has 7 tens.

7   70   700   7,000

D

(7   2   4)

Order the three numerals to make the largest and smallest numbers possible.

largest _____

smallest _____

How do you know?

_____

E

Skip count by

2s   96, ____, ____, ____, ____

5s   115, ____, ____, ____, ____

10s   343, ____, ____, ____, ____

100s 82, ____, ____, ____, ____

F

Write the number shown in

standard form _____

word form _____

expanded form _____

G

Use **<**, **>**, or **=** to compare.

1. 120 ◯ 12   **2.** 712 ◯ 232

3. 901 ◯ 901   **4.** 417 ◯ 471

5. 19 ◯ 185   **6.** 563 ◯ 582

H

Order each set from least to greatest.

(871   868   87   817)

_____

(511   541   514   504)

_____

Solve.

45	80	52	41
+ 31	+ 17	+ 37	+ 26

I

Solve.

98	63	47	75
− 33	− 43	− 12	− 53

J

Solve.

36	81	77	65
+ 46	+ 43	+ 23	+ 75

K

Solve.

80	74	68	50
− 14	− 58	− 29	− 37

L

Look at the problem.
Is the answer correct?

yes   no

If not, correct it.

347
+ 288
525

M

Look at the problem.
Is the answer correct?

yes   no

If not, correct it.

804
− 452
452

N

Solve.

23	62	28	41
16	44	11	17
+ 30	+ 21	55	22
		+ 32	+ 35

O

862 − 10 = _____

Use the answer above to solve this problem.

862 − 40 = _____

How did the first problem help you solve the second problem? _____

_____

P

Name _____   Date _____

✦ Show What You Know ✦
Measurement and Data

1. Circle the best tool for measuring the length of each object.

leaf

ruler   meterstick   tape measure

- -

car

ruler   meterstick   tape measure

- -

sidewalk

ruler   meterstick   tape measure

2. Measure the rocket to the nearest inch and centimeter.

_____ in.

_____ cm

3. Look at your answer to problem 2. Are there more inches or centimeters? Why?

_____

_____

_____

_____

4. Estimate the length of each object. Then, measure it to the nearest centimeter.

Estimate: _____ cm   _____ cm

Actual: _____ cm   _____ cm

5. Which object in problem 4 is longer?

_____

How much longer? _____

6. Claire planted a sunflower. After three weeks, it was 11 inches tall. After eight weeks, it was 50 inches tall. How much did the sunflower grow between three and eight weeks?

A. 61 inches

B. 41 inches

C. 50 inches

D. 39 inches

7. Draw hands on the clock to show 3:40.

8. What time is it?

_____

9. Hector has 2 quarters, 3 dimes, and 3 pennies. He finds 2 nickels. How much money does he have now?

10. Ellis measured the heights of his action figures in centimeters.

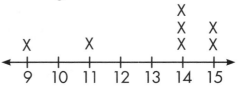

He bought a new action figure that is 13 centimeters tall. Add it to the line plot.

How many action figures does Ellis have that are taller than 14 centimeters? _____

11.

Animals Dawn Saw

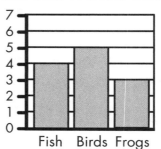

Did Dawn see more fish or birds on her hike? _____

12.

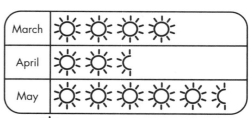

☀ = 4 sunny days

How many days were sunny in both March and April? _____

Name _____ Date _____

✦ Show What You Know ✦
Measurement and Data

1. Circle the best tool for measuring the length of each object.

a room

ruler   meterstick   tape measure

- -

beetle

ruler   meterstick   tape measure

- -

table

ruler   meterstick   tape measure

2. Measure the building to the nearest inch and centimeter.

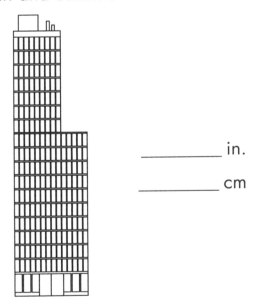

_____ in.

_____ cm

3. Look at your answer to problem 2. Why are the amounts different?

_____

_____

4. Estimate the length of each object. Then, measure it to the nearest centimeter.

Estimate: _____ cm _____ cm

Actual: _____ cm _____ cm

5. Which object in problem 4 is shorter?

_____

How much shorter? _____

6. Leo needs to wrap a present. He wraps 73 centimeters of ribbon around the box. He uses 18 centimeters more to make a bow. How much ribbon did he use in all?

A. 55 centimeters

B. 91 centimeters

C. 81 centimeters

D. 100 centimeters

7. Draw hands on the clock to show 9:25.

8. What time is it?

_____

9. Paige has 1 quarter, 4 nickels, and 1 penny. Her grandmother gives her 2 dimes and a nickel. How much money does she have now?

10. Morgan measured the lengths of bugs in centimeters.

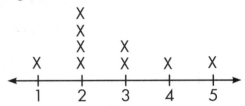

What was the most common length

Morgan measured? _____

11. **Favorite Colors**

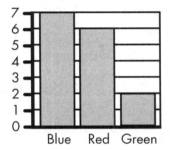

How many people voted in all? _____

12.

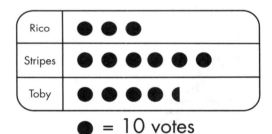

● = 10 votes

Vale Elementary is naming their mascot, a tiger.

After absent students voted, there were 5 more votes for Rico. Add them to the picture graph.

How many students voted for the name Toby?

_____

Units of Length

Circle the best tool for measuring the length of each object.

1. ![feather] ruler   meterstick   tape measure

2. ![pool] ruler   meterstick   tape measure

3. ![bracelet] ruler   meterstick   tape measure

4. ![rug] ruler   meterstick   tape measure

Circle the best measurement.

5.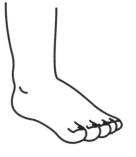

8 inches

8 feet

6.

4 inches

4 feet

7.

15 centimeters

15 meters

8.

3 centimeters

3 meters

9.

6 feet

6 yards

10.

12 inches

12 feet

Measuring Length

Measure each line to the nearest inch or centimeter. Record the length.

1. ——————————— This line is _____ inches long.

2. ————— This line is _____ centimeters long.

3. ————————————————

This line is _____ inches long.

4. ———————————— This line is _____ centimeters long.

5. ——————————————————

This line is _____ inches long.

6. ————————————————

This line is _____ inches long.

7. ——————————————————

This line is _____ centimeters long.

8. ——————————————

This line is _____ centimeters long.

9. ———— This line is _____ inches long.

10. ———————————————— This line is _____ centimeters long.

Measuring Length and Width

Use these cards to assess a student's proficiency with measuring objects. Provide a student with a card or set of cards and have him use a ruler to measure the item to the nearest whole unit (centimeters or inches). Some items can be measured in both directions, such as the robot.

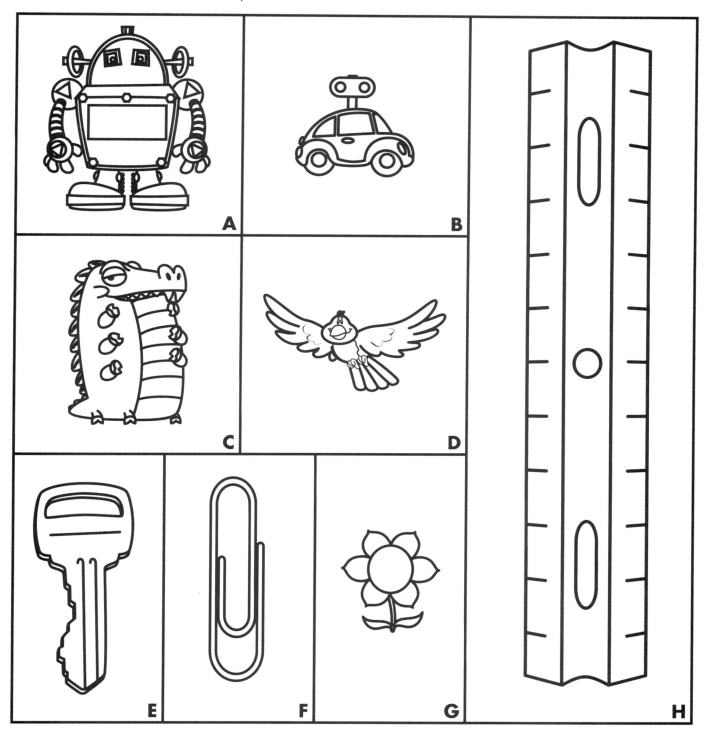

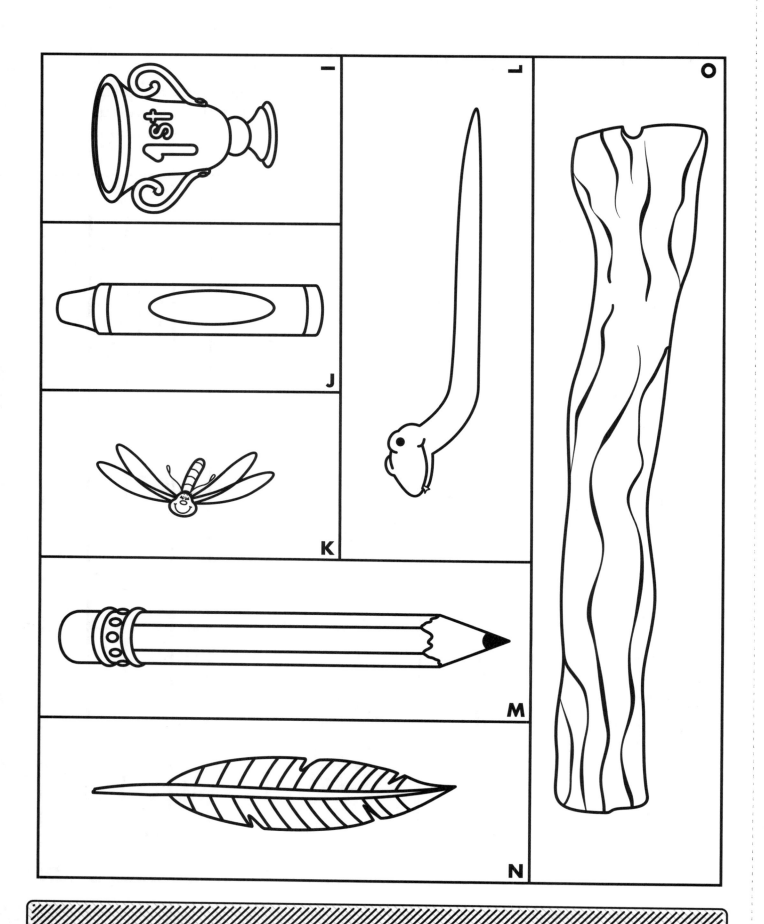

Comparing Units

Measure each object to the nearest whole unit. Write the length in inches and centimeters.

1. 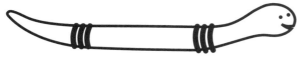   _____ in.

_____ cm

2.    _____ in.

_____ cm

3.    _____ in.

_____ cm

4.    _____ in.

_____ cm

5. 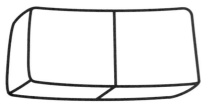   _____ in.

_____ cm

6. Tell what you notice about the measurements in centimeters compared to inches.

_____

7. This bandage measures about 3 inches. Do you think it will measure greater than or less than 3 centimeters?

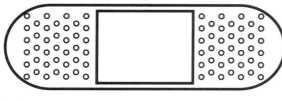   greater than 3 cm

less than 3 cm

Why?

_____

Name _____ Date _____

Estimating Lengths

Estimate the length of each line using the unit given. Record it in the **Estimate** column. Then, measure each line. Record the measurement in the **Actual** column.

	Estimate	Actual
1. ————————————	——— in.	——— in.
2. ———	——— in.	——— in.
3. —————	——— in.	——— in.
4. ————————————	——— in.	——— in.
5. —————	——— in.	——— in.
6. ———————————	——— cm	——— cm
7. ———————————	——— cm	——— cm
8. ———	——— cm	——— cm
9. ————————————	——— cm	——— cm
10. ———————	——— cm	——— cm

Comparing Lengths

Measure each object to the nearest inch or centimeter. Use the measurements to answer the questions.

1.

_____ cm

_____ cm

How much longer is the ticket than the stick of gum? _____

2.

_____ in.

_____ in.

How much longer is the feather than the leaf? _____

3.

_____ cm

_____ cm

How much longer is the candy than the coin? _____

Name _____ Date _____

Length Word Problems

Read each problem. Solve.

1. A cat climbed to the top of a 50-foot-tall tree. Wyatt's dad has climbed 31 feet up the tree so far. How much farther does he need to climb?

2. Miranda has 14 inches of border. She needs 31 inches for a bulletin board. How much more border does Miranda need to finish the bulletin board?

3. Becca measured 34 inches of plastic track for a race track. She wants to add 57 more inches. How long will the race track be?

4. Nina made a scarf that was 97 centimeters long. It was too short, so she added 85 centimeters more. How long is the scarf now?

5. Julio bought a 25 centimeter collar for his puppy. He had to shorten it by 9 centimeters. How long is the collar now?

6. Two fishermen traveled 82 meters down a creek. Later in the day, they went 79 meters farther. How far did they travel in all?

Lengths on a Number Line

Show each length on a number line.

1. 7 inches

2. 12 yards

3. 19 centimeters

Solve each word problem using the number line.

4. Kelly had 19 feet of ribbon. She gave Chris 7 feet. How much ribbon does she have left?

 _____ feet

5. Paul had 18 meters of fishing line. Then, 11 meters broke off. How many meters are left?

 _____ meters

6. Delia has 7 yards of kite string. She needs 12 more yards. How many yards does she need altogether?

 _____ yards

Time

Write each time.

1.

_____

2.

_____

3.

_____

Draw hands on each clock to match the time.

4. 2:35

5. 5:05

6. 10:10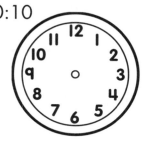

Color the clocks that have matching digital and analog time.

7.

| 12:10 |

| 3:25 |

| 6:20 |

| 9:50 |

Circle **am** or **pm** to show the best time for each activity.

8. going on a bike ride at 3:30   **am**   **pm**

9. picking strawberries at 10:30   **am**   **pm**

10. Avery had to be home by 6:00. If she walked in the door at the time shown on the clock, is Avery on time, late, or early?

_____

Time

Use these cards to assess a student's understanding of time concepts. You can present a student with each card and have her tell the time, say a time and have her find the matching clock, or have her match analog clocks to digital clocks (each analog clock has a matching digital time). Or, to assess a student's understanding of *am* and *pm*, present a scenario, such as *When would you eat lunch?* and have her choose a reasonable time and the *am* or *pm* card.

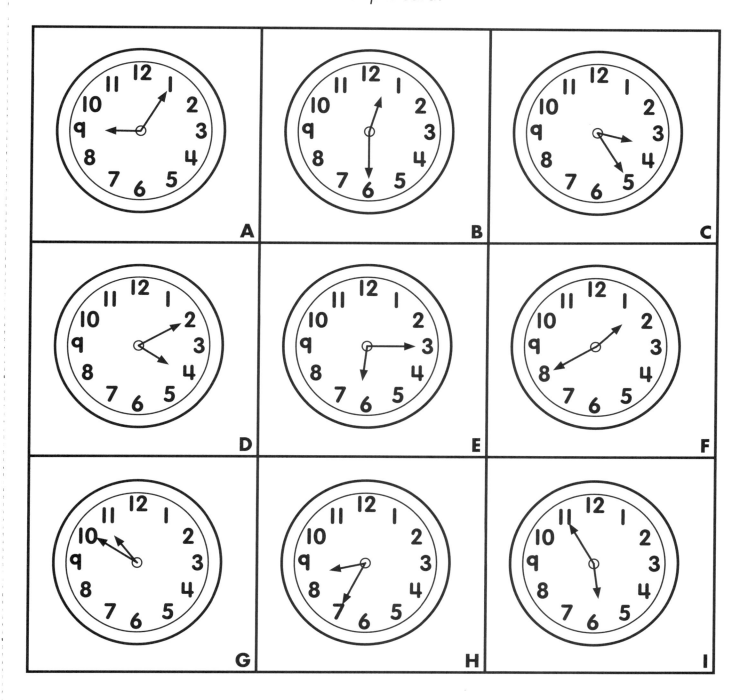

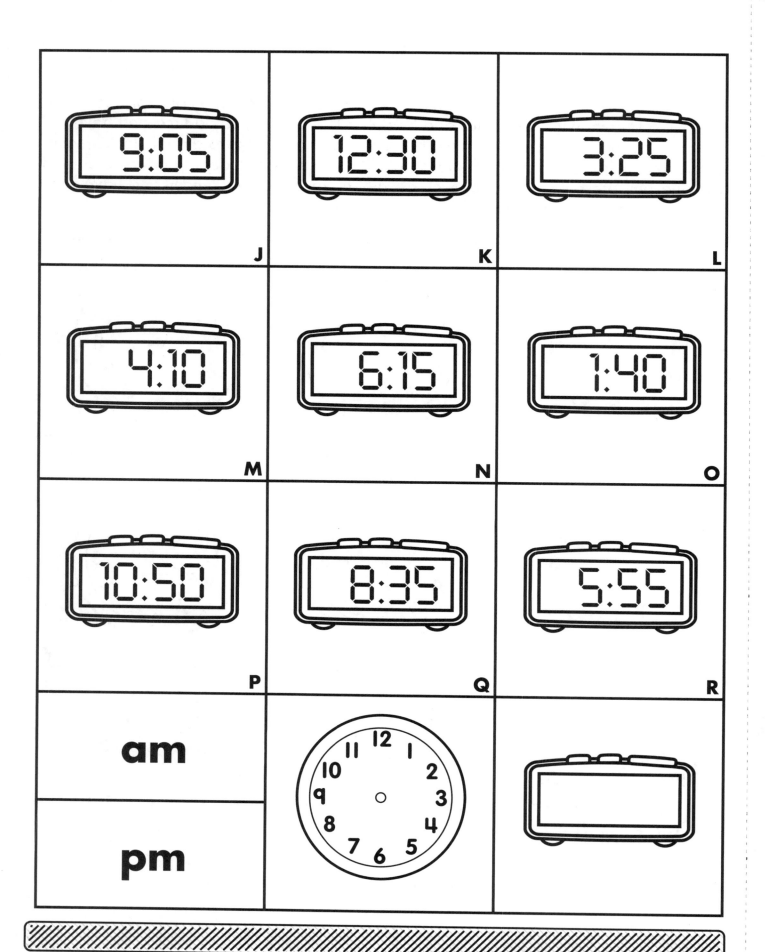

Money

Use these cards to assess a student's understanding of money concepts. Present several cards to a student and have him tell the total amount shown, show the same amount with a different set of coins, or use two cards together to create a word problem. For example, *Pablo has this much money* (show card C). *He finds more money in a drawer* (show card F). *How much money does he have now?*

25¢ 10¢ 5¢ 1¢ **A**	25¢ 25¢ 5¢ 5¢ 5¢ 1¢ 1¢ 1¢ 1¢ **B**
25¢ 25¢ 25¢ 25¢ 25¢ 25¢ 10¢ 1¢ **C**	10¢ 10¢ 10¢ 10¢ 10¢ 10¢ 10¢ 10¢ 10¢ 1¢ 1¢ 1¢ **D**
25¢ 25¢ 25¢ 10¢ 10¢ 1¢ **E**	25¢ 25¢ 5¢ 5¢ 5¢ 5¢ 5¢ 5¢ **F**

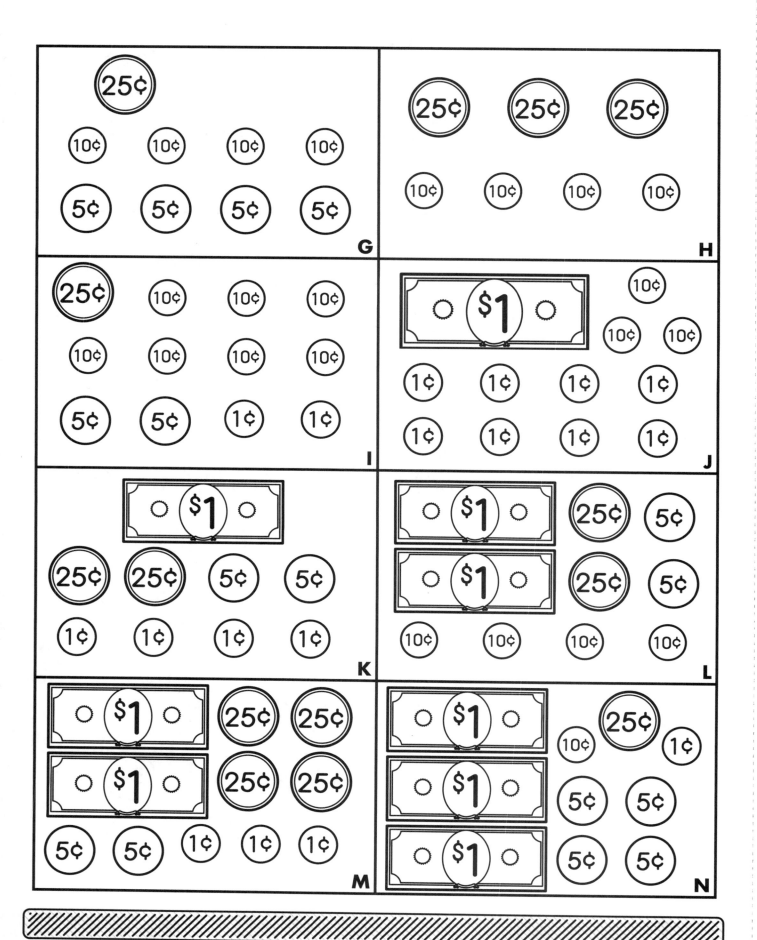

Money

Write how many of each coin you need to equal each amount.

1. 5¢

_____ nickel or

_____ pennies

2. 10¢

_____ dime or

_____ nickels or

_____ pennies

3. 25¢

_____ quarter or

_____ nickels or

_____ pennies

4. 50¢

_____ quarters or

_____ dimes or

_____ nickels

5. $1.00

_____ quarters or

_____ nickels or

_____ dimes or

_____ pennies

Find the total value.

6. $ _____

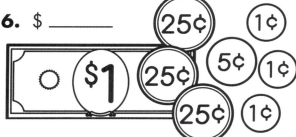

7. $ _____

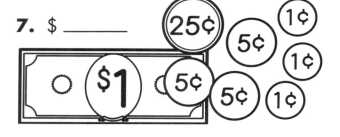

Draw coins and dollar bills to show each amount.

8. 79¢

9. $1.08

10. Greg has 85¢. He has 4 dimes. What could the other coins be?

_____

Money Word Problems

Read each problem. Solve.

1. Amber has 63¢. She found 2 dimes and a penny on her walk. How much money does she have now?	**2.** Kenan had 80¢ in his pocket. He lost 2 dimes and 3 pennies through a hole in his pocket. How much money does he have left?
3. Michelle has 7 dimes. Lynn gives her 1 nickel and 2 pennies. How much money does Michelle have now?	**4.** Thad has $1.18. He earns 75¢ doing chores. How much money does Thad have now?
5. Ruby had $1.50 in her backpack. She lost 42¢. How much money does she have left?	**6.** Reese has 2 quarters, 1 dime, and 1 penny. Sean has 1 quarter, 4 dimes, and 1 penny. Who has more money? How much more?

Name _____ Date _____

Interpreting Line Plots

The line plot shows the heights in inches of the books on Jamie's shelf. Use the line plot to answer the questions.

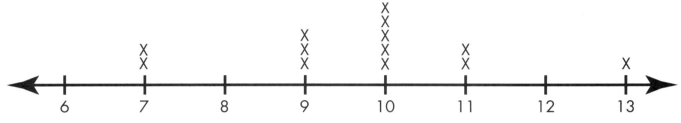

1. What is the most common height of the books? _____

2. How many books are 11 inches tall? _____

3. How many books are 8 inches tall? _____

4. Which height shows three books? _____

5. Jamie measured two more books. The first one was 7 inches high and the second one was 12 inches high. Mark Xs on the line plot to add the books to the graph.

The line plot shows the lengths in centimeters of the caterpillars Noah measured. Use the line plot to answer the questions.

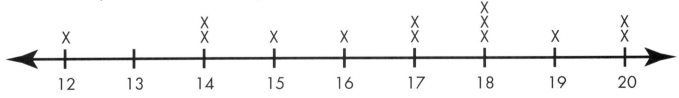

6. How many caterpillars did Noah measure in all? _____

7. Noah found 0 caterpillars that were how long? _____

8. Write one true statement about the line plot.

_____

_____

Making and Interpreting Line Plots

Mr. Hansen's class made bookmarks of different lengths to sell at the school festival.

Lengths of Bookmarks

16 cm	18 cm
21 cm	15 cm
15 cm	16 cm
17 cm	16 cm
18 cm	16 cm

Use the data to complete the line plot. Then, answer the questions.

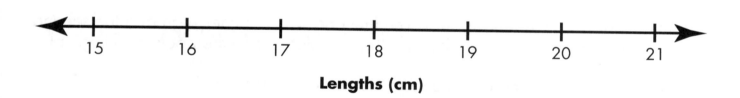

Lengths (cm)

1. How many 15-centimeter bookmarks did the class make? _____

2. Which length had the most bookmarks? _____

3. How many more bookmarks were 16 centimeters than 18 centimeters?

_____

4. Mason made one more bookmark that was 20 centimeters long. Graph that bookmark on the line plot.

5. How many bookmarks did the class make in all? _____

Interpreting Bar Graphs

After a field trip, students voted for their favorite zoo exhibit. Use the graph to answer the questions.

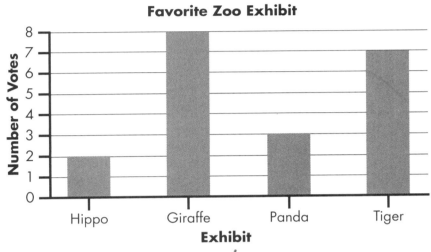

Favorite Zoo Exhibit

1. Which exhibit got the most votes? _Giraffe_____

How many students voted for that exhibit? _____

2. How many more students liked the giraffe exhibit than the hippo exhibit?

_____

3. How many students liked the giraffe and tiger exhibits in all? _____

4. How many students voted in all? _____
How do you know?

_____

_____

5. Which exhibit was more popular—the panda or the tiger? _____
How can you tell?

_____

_____

Making and Interpreting Bar Graphs

Look at the tables. Create bar graphs from the data. Then, use the graphs to answer the questions.

Dessert	Total Orders
Brownie	10
Cupcake	6
Pie	9

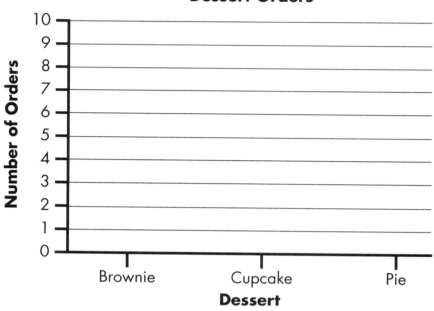

Dessert Orders

1. Which dessert was ordered the most? _____

2. How many more customers ordered a brownie than pie? _____

3. How many total customers ordered a cupcake or pie? _____

Student	Books Read
Erica	12
Hugo	8
Amy	9
John	5

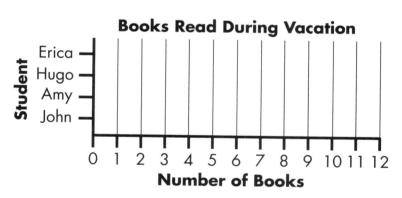

Books Read During Vacation

4. Who read the least amount of books? _____

5. How many more books did Erica read than John? _____

6. How many books did the students read in all? _____

Interpreting Picture Graphs

Four students planted tomato seeds. Use the graph to answer the questions.

Tomato Seeds Planted

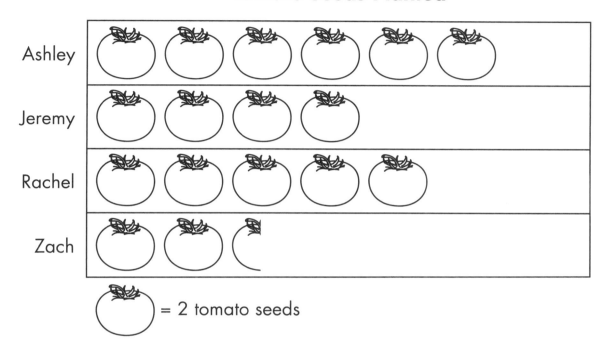

= 2 tomato seeds

1. Which student planted the most seeds? _____

2. How many seeds did Rachel plant?_____

3. Who planted more seeds—Jeremy or Rachel? _____

How many more? _____

4. Which student planted 5 tomato seeds? _____

5. How many seeds did Jeremy and Rachel plant together? _____

6. Jo says the students planted 17 seeds in all. Is she right? _____

Why or why not?

_____

_____

Making and Interpreting
Picture Graphs

Look at the tables. Create pictures graphs from the data. Then, use the graphs to answer the questions.

Activity	Number of Students
Read	8
Dice math	9
Color	12
Clean desk	5

Choice Time

Activity	Number of Students
Read	
Dice math	
Color	
Clean desk	

Key ◯ = _____

1. If 10 students made an art project, how many circles would you draw? _____

2. Circle **T** for true or **F** for false.

    T   F   More students chose reading than cleaning their desk.

    T   F   An equal number of students did dice math and read.

    T   F   The least amount of students cleaned their desks.

    T   F   Three more students colored than did dice math.

Item	Amount Recycled
Glass bottles	40
Aluminum cans	55
Newspapers	20
Plastic containers	60

Neighborhood Recycling—Week 1

Item	Amount Recycled
Glass bottles	
Aluminum cans	
Newspapers	
Plastic containers	

Key △ = _____

3. Explain why you chose they key you did. _____

_____

4. How many more cans were recycled than bottles? _____

5. How many items were recycled altogether? _____

A. Choose the best tool to measure each object.

butterfly

meterstick   ruler   tape measure

car length

meterstick   ruler   tape measure

desk height

meterstick   ruler   tape measure

B. Circle the best measurement for each item.

height of a dog

19 inches   19 feet

length of a pool

8 centimeters   8 meters

width of a car

6 feet   6 yards

C. Measure to the nearest centimeter.

height

_____ cm

width

_____ cm

D. Measure to the nearest inch.

height

_____ in.

width

_____ in.

E. Measure to the nearest centimeter and inch.

_____ cm   _____ in.

Why are the measurements different?

_____

_____

F. Measure both objects to the nearest centimeter. How much longer is the snake than the worm?

_____

G. Solve.

Kennedy is practicing on her skateboard. On her first try, she rode 52 feet before falling off. On her second try, she rode 71 feet. How much longer did she ride the second time?

H.

A at 32, B at 39 on number line: 30 31 32 33 34 35 36 37 38 39 40

How far is it from A to B? _____

How do you know? _____

_____

I. Match each clock to the correct time.

4:45

11:05

5:10

6:20

J. Complete the time on each blank clock to match the other time.

07:25

K. Count each set of money. Write the amount.

25¢ 25¢ 25¢
10¢ 5¢ 5¢ 5¢
1¢

$1
10¢ 10¢ 10¢ 10¢
5¢ 5¢ 1¢ 1¢

_____   _____

L. Solve.

Patrick has saved $3.50 so far. Last week he found 1 quarter, 2 dimes, and 6 pennies on the ground. How much money does Patrick have now?

M. Draw coins to show $1.36.

N. Lucy recorded how many pieces of pepperoni each slice of a pizza had. Use her data to complete the line plot.

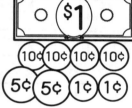

2   3   3   5   2   4   3

⟵―――――――――――――――――⟶

O.

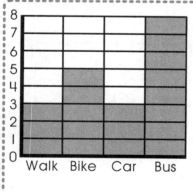

How many more people take the bus than walk to school?

_____

P.

December	❄ ❄ ⟩
January	❄ ❄ ❄ ❄ ❄ ❄
February	❄ ❄ ❄ ❄ ❄ ❄ ⟩

❄ = 2 snowy days

How many snowy days were there in both December and January? _____

✦ Show What You Know ✦
Geometry

1. Draw a shape that is a hexagon.

Draw a shape that is not a hexagon.

What is a hexagon?

_____

_____

2. A triangle has _____ angles and

a quadrilateral has _____ angles.

3. What is a shape with five sides
called?

A. triangle

B. parallelogram

C. pentagon

D. hexagon

4. Divide the rectangle into 2 rows and
5 columns.

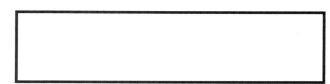

How many equal-sized parts are

there? _____

5. Divide the circle into 4 equal shares.

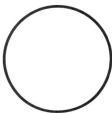

Name the shares. _____

6. Which shape shows halves?

A.

B.

C.

D.

Name _____ Date _____

✦ Show What You Know ✦
Geometry

1. Draw a shape that is a quadrilateral.

Draw a shape that is not a quadrilateral.

What is a quadrilateral?

_____

_____

2. A pentagon has _____ sides and

a hexagon has _____ sides.

3. What is a shape with three angles called?

A. triangle

B. trapezoid

C. quadrilateral

D. hexagon

4. Divide the rectangle into 4 rows and 2 columns.

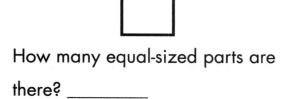

How many equal-sized parts are

there? _____

5. Divide the square into 2 equal shares.

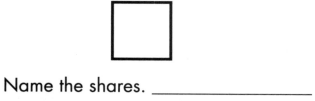

Name the shares. _____

6. Which shape shows thirds?

A.

B.

C.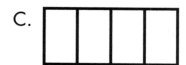

D.

Geometric Figures

Use these cards to assess students' proficiency with geometric figures and their attributes. You can have a student match shapes to names, sort by common attributes, or present a figure and have her describe all of its attributes. You can also present several figures and have her explain what attributes they share and how they are different, or lay out all of the cards and have her find all of the shapes with a specified attribute.

	cube	
triangle		hexagon
	quadrilateral	

square		rectangle
	trapezoid	
rhombus		parallelogram
	pentagon	

Shape Attributes

Name each shape. Then, tell how many sides and angles.

1.  _____

_____ sides

_____ angles

2. 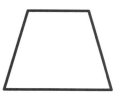 _____

_____ sides

_____ angles

3. 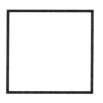 _____

_____ sides

_____ angles

4.  _____

_____ sides

_____ angles

Draw two different examples of each shape.

5. triangle	**6.** hexagon	**7.** parallelogram	**8.** rectangle

9. Look at the shapes. Draw an **X** on the shape or shapes that do not belong.

How are the rest of the shapes the same?

_____

10. Andrew and Pilar both drew a pentagon.

Andrew 　　　　Pilar

Andrew says that only his shape is a pentagon. Is he right? Why or why not?

_____

_____

Name _____ Date _____

Partitioning

1. Divide this rectangle into 2 rows and 4 columns.

How many parts are there? _____

2. Divide this rectangle into 3 rows and 3 columns.

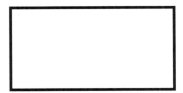

How many parts are there? _____

3. Divide each shape into two equal shares. Circle the name of the parts.

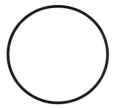 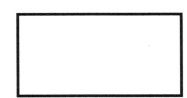

halves

thirds

fourths

4. Divide each shape into four equal shares. Circle the name of the parts.

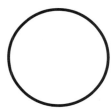 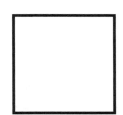

halves

thirds

fourths

5. Divide each rectangle into fourths a different way.

 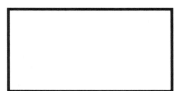 

Are the parts equal? Why or why not? _____

_____

Partitioning Shapes

Use these cards to assess a student's understanding of partitioning shapes. You can present the student with a card and ask him to describe the shares, have him sort all of the cards under the proper headers (using the *halves*, *thirds*, and *fourths* cards), or show him two cards and have him describe how the partitioning is the same or different and why.

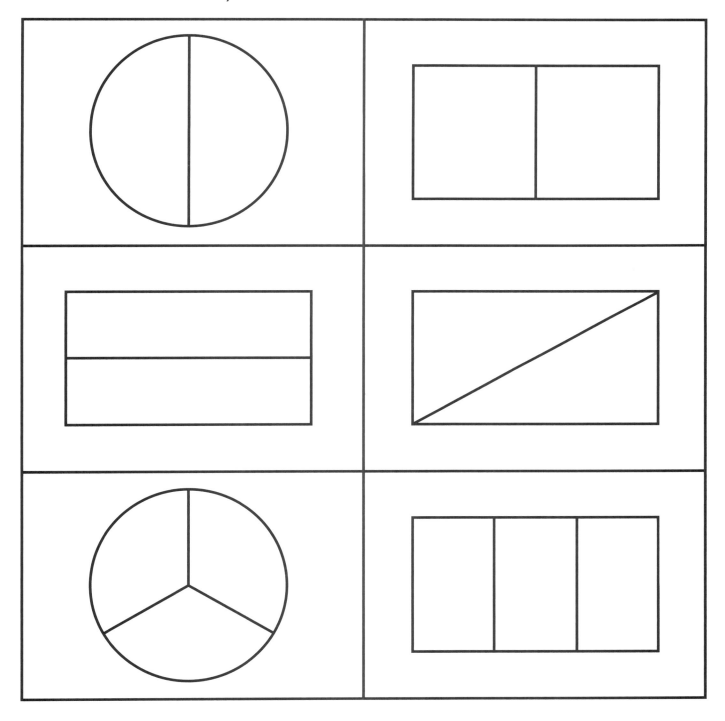

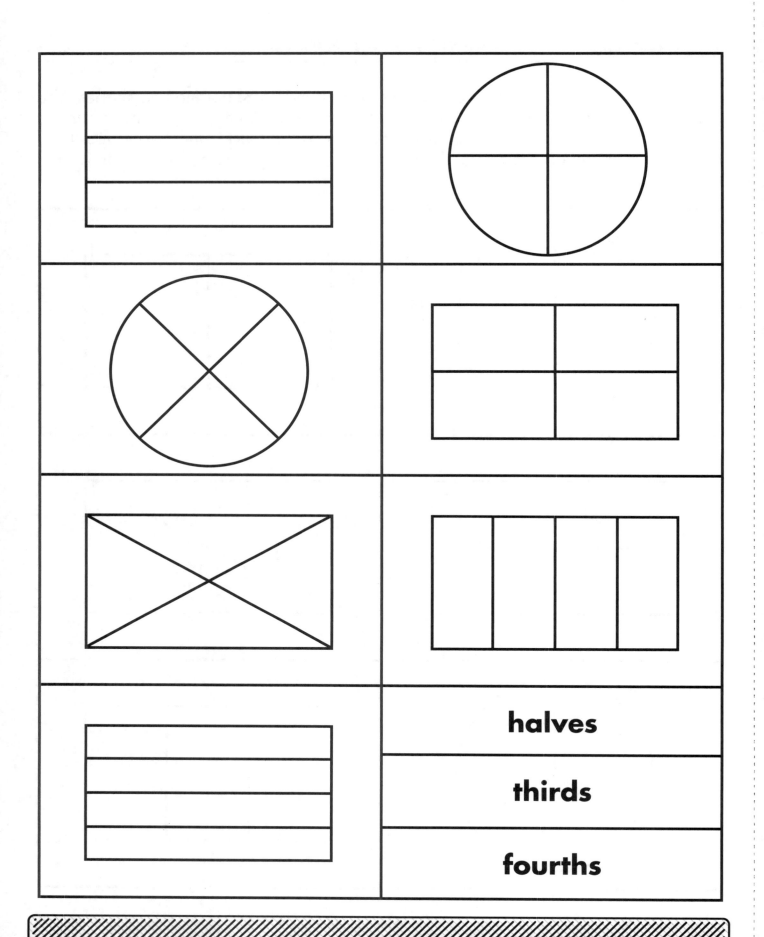

halves

thirds

fourths

A

Circle the triangle.

- -

Draw a different triangle.

B

What shape has four sides and four angles?

triangle   quadrilateral   pentagon

How many angles in a pentagon?

4   5   6

How many sides on a hexagon?

4   5   6

C

Draw and name two different quadrilaterals.

_____   _____

D

Draw an **X** on the shapes that are not cubes.

How do you know? _____

_____

E

Color the quadrilaterals.

How do you know? _____

_____

F

Color the triangles blue, the quadrilaterals yellow, the pentagons red, and the hexagons green.

G

Divide the rectangle into 4 rows and 3 columns.

H

Divide the rectangle into 3 rows and 2 columns.

Divide the rectangle into 3 rows and 4 columns.

How many squares are there? _____ **I**

Brian must draw the same-size squares to fill the rectangle. Help him draw the squares. How many square units are there altogether?

There are _____ square units. **J**

Divide the circles to show equal and not equal shares.

equal   **not equal** **K**

Partition each shape into three equal shares. **L**

Partition each shape into four equal shares. **M**

Circle the name of each share shown.

1. halves
       thirds
       fourths

2. halves
       thirds
       fourths

3. halves
       thirds
       fourths

4. halves
       thirds
       fourths **N**

Do both rectangles show the same shares?   **yes**   **no**

Why or why not? _____

_____ **O**

Partition each rectangle into halves a different way. **P**

Answer Key

Pages 11–12
1. even; 2. even, odd, odd; 3. 3 + 3, 7 + 7, 10 + 10; 4. 16, 4 + 4 + 4 + 4 =16; 5. 37 pages; 6. 26 lb.; 7. 23 books; 8. 15, 8, 10, 9, 3; 9. 4, 0, 12, 12, 9; 10. 11, 2, 7, 4, 8; 11. 5, 10, 8, 8, 0; 12. 2, 10, 8, 7, 5

Pages 13–14
1. odd; 2. even, odd, even; 3. 4 + 4, 8 + 8, 6 + 6; 4. 15, 5 + 5 + 5 = 15; 5. 99 trees; 6. 34 rows ; 7. 12 pages; 8. 6, 7, 8, 10, 10; 9. 9, 5, 9, 13, 9; 10. 7, 13, 9, 3, 7; 11. 6, 1, 7, 4, 7; 12. 10, 8, 11, 5, 3

Pages 15–18
A. 23 businesses; B. 33 items; C. 47 desks; D. 73 fans; E. 76 min.; F. 105 beads; G. 88 peaches; H. 82 students; I. 61 items; J. 87 cupcakes; K. 9 bracelets; L. 4 swings; M. 16 cupcakes; N. 12 cherry tomatoes; O. 17 slices; P. 24 stamps; Q. 25 rectangular prisms; R. 33 min.; S. 46 fish; T. 59 pages; U. 15 eggs; V. 31 action figures; W. 62 scoops; X. 65 min.; Y. 6 pages; Z. $57; AA. 36 oz.; AB. 25 vegetables; AC. 60¢; AD. Yes, she lost 5.

Page 19
Even: B, D, F, G, I; Odd: A, C, E, H

Page 20
1. Check students' coloring. 2. Answers will vary but may include that even numbers end in 0, 2, 4, 6, or 8 and odd numbers end in 1, 3, 5, 7, or 9. 3. Even: 40, 52, 68, 74, 96; Odd: 23, 31, 37, 49, 85; 4. 4, 4; 5. 7, 7; 6. 6, 6; 7. 2, 2; 8. 5, 5; 9. 3, 3; 10. Answers will vary.

Page 23
1. 4 + 4 + 4 + 4 = 16; 2. 2 + 2 + 2 + 2 + 2 = 10 or 5 + 5 = 10; 3. 5 + 5 + 5 = 15 or 3 + 3 + 3 + 3 + 3 = 15; 4. 2 + 2 + 2 + 2 = 8 or 4 + 4 = 8; 5. 5 + 5 + 5 + 5 = 20 or 4 + 4 + 4 + 4 + 4 = 20; 6. 3 + 3 + 3 + 3 =12 or 4 + 4 + 4 = 12; 7. 3 + 3 = 6 or 2 + 2 + 2 = 6; 8. 3 + 3 + 3 = 9; 9. 12, Check students' work. 10. 10, Check students' work.

Page 24
1. 8, 6, 7, 11, 5; 2. 6, 12, 11, 7, 4; 3. 12, 3, 7, 9, 7; 4. 2, 5, 4, 10, 9; 5. 12, 8, 9, 5, 5; 6. 10, 17, 4, 5, 5; 7. 7, 5, 6, 13, 9; 8. 0, 14, 7, 3, 6; 9. 7, 15, 9, 16, 3; 10. 8, 8, 5, 9, 14

Pages 25–26
A. –, Answers will vary. B. 7 + ? = 13; C. 27 birds; D. yes, 11 points; E. 1. 2; 2. 7; 3. 13; 4. 12; 5. 7; 6. 15; 7. 14; 8. 10; F. 1. 6; 2. 5; 3. 8; 4. 6; 5. 15; 6. 9; 7. 10; 8. 16; G. 20, 11; H. 15, 18; I. odd, even, even; J. 1. even; 2. odd; 3. odd; 4. even; 5. even; 6. even; 7. odd; 8. odd; K. 10 + 10 = 20, 8 + 8 = 16; L. circled: 3 + 9, 2 + 6, 6 + 10; boxed: 1 + 4, 8 + 5, 7 + 6; M. 12; N. no, Answers will vary. O. 4 + 4 + 4 + 4 + 4 = 20 or 5 + 5 + 5 + 5 = 20; P. Check students' drawings.

Pages 27–28
1. 264; 2. 9, 800, 60; 3. >, <, <; 4. 234, 345, 354, 432; 5. 700 + 4, seven hundred four; 6. 400 + 50 + 9, four hundred fifty-nine; 7. 130, 135; 88, 108; 417, 717; 8. 30 lemons; 9. 98; 10. 58; 11. 96; 12. 101; 13. 569; 14. 773; 15. 783; 16. 1,082; 17. 31; 18. 43; 19. 37; 20. 28; 21. 412; 22. 332; 23. 156; 24. 60; 25. 549; 26. 216; 27. 921; 28. 285

Answer Key

Pages 29–30
1. 342; 2. 3, 200, 40; 3. <, <, <; 4. 220, 251, 520, 552; 5. 600 + 40 + 3, six hundred forty-three; 6. 800 + 5, eight hundred five; 7. 570, 580; 132, 142; 674, 974; 8. 70 people; 9. 67; 10. 97; 11. 73; 12. 121; 13. 858; 14. 779; 15. 761; 16. 1,040; 17. 54; 18. 51; 19. 11; 20. 17; 21. 236; 22. 123; 23. 189; 24. 258; 25. 326; 26. 582; 27. 760; 28. 373

Pages 31–32
A. 800; B. 170; C. 510; D. 420; E. 241; F. 341; G. 276; H. 192; I. 309; J. 539; K. 703; L. 285; M. 624; N. 408

Page 33
1. 2, 7, 7, 277; 2. 6, 1, 8, 618; 3. 204; 4. 511; 5. 5; 6. 300; 7. 40; 8. 8; 9. 853, 358; 10. Check students' work.

Page 34
1. 255, 260, 265; 2. 595, 610, 625; 3. 470, 480, 490; 4. 235, 255, 265; 5. 763, 863, 963; 6. 321, 421, 621; 7. 30; 8. 35; 9. 12; 10. circled: 43, 51; corrected: 44, 50

Page 35
1. 362, 300 + 60 + 2, three hundred sixty-two; 2. 507, 500 + 7, five hundred seven; 3. 714; 4. 267; 5. 910; 6. 478; 7. 812; 8. 195; 9. 700 + 30 + 4; 10. 600 + 1; 11. nine hundred seventy-five; 12. eight hundred thirty

Page 36
1. >; 2. <; 3. =; 4. <; 5. >; 6. <; 7. 52; 8. 727; 9. 274; 10. 888; 11. 194; 12. 334; 13. 91, 111, 121, 131; 14. 601, 610, 623, 632; 15. Answers will vary but should include that the hundreds place is greater in 540.

Pages 37–38
Regrouping: B, E, G, H, J, K, M, N, Q, S, U; No regrouping: A, C, D, F, I, L, O, P, R, T; A. 68; B. 90; C. 97; D. 69; E. 93; F. 87; G. 129; H. 120; I. 88; J. 41; K. 59; L. 74; M. 19; N. 47; O. 20; P. 21; Q. 38; R. 71; S. 18; T. 22; U. 46

Page 39
1. 89; 2. 99; 3. 48; 4. 87; 5. 68; 6. 91; 7. 68; 8. 99; 9. 97; 10. 75; 11. 79; 12. 89; 13. 94; 14. 85; 15. 89; 16. 97; 17. 98; 18. 56; 19. 87; 20. 99

Page 40
1. 62; 2. 41; 3. 100; 4. 61; 5. 82; 6. 81; 7. 101; 8. 71; 9. 92; 10. 100; 11. 43; 12. 120; 13. 73; 14. 111; 15. 122; 16. 92; 17. 54; 18. 67; 19. 81; 20. 61

Page 41
1. 73; 2. 106; 3. 139; 4. 170; 5. 112; 6. 125; 7. 134; 8. 151; 9. 117; 10. 169

Page 42
1. 72; 2. 74; 3. 42; 4. 62; 5. 32; 6. 44; 7. 11; 8. 53; 9. 21; 10. 40; 11. 14; 12. 34; 13. 41; 14. 31; 15. 21; 16. 44; 17. 34; 18. 25; 19. 12; 20. 17

Page 43
1. 28; 2. 8; 3. 39; 4. 7; 5. 19; 6. 7; 7. 14; 8. 69; 9. 15; 10. 16; 11. 68; 12. 15; 13. 38; 14. 56; 15. 13; 16. 29; 17. 15; 18. 3; 19. 17; 20. 57

Page 44
1. 9; 2. 49; 3. 89; 4. 17; 5. 90; 6. 65; 7. 87; 8. 14; 9. 44; 10. 161; 11. 28; 12. 83; 13. 69; 14. 34; 15. 24; 16. 101; 17. 44; 18. 13; 19. 165; 20. 65

Answer Key

Page 45
1. 725; 2 849; 3. 399; 4. 898; 5. 979;
6. 395; 7. 689; 8. 776; 9. 484; 10. 297;
11. 797; 12. 988; 13. 694; 14. 835;
15. 389; 16. 987; 17. 773; 18. 988;
19. 888; 20. 569

Page 46
1. 820; 2. 457; 3. 731; 4. 622; 5. 871;
6. 863; 7. 564; 8. 1,050; 9. 1,271; 10. 557;
11. 1,032; 12. 598; 13. 1.252; 14. 801;
15. 1,013; 16. 670; 17. 951; 18. 791;
19. 732; 20. 702

Page 47
1. 447; 2. 135; 3. 25; 4. 121; 5. 261;
6. 521; 7. 311; 8. 435; 9. 184; 10. 345;
11. 342; 12. 213; 13. 214; 14. 320; 15. 72;
16. 162; 17. 243; 18. 53; 19. 313; 20. 331

Page 48
1. 112; 2. 489; 3. 308; 4. 284; 5. 245;
6. 288; 7. 689; 8. 112; 9. 174; 10. 546;
11. 185; 12. 188; 13. 452; 14. 299;
15. 498; 16. 379; 17. 345; 18. 98; 19. 159;
20. 187

Page 49
1. 872; 2. 590; 3. 243; 4. 693; 5. 830;
6. 330; 7. 875; 8. 187; 9. 236; 10. 425;
11. 279; 12. 1,083; 13. 883; 14. 223;
15. 169; 16. 711; 17. 654; 18. 992; 19. 43;
20. 702

Page 50
1. 1, 21; 2. 43, 63; 3. 84, 104; 4. 391, 591;
5. 562, 762; 6. 708, 908; 7. 78; 8. 47;
9. 361; 10. 41; 11. 72; 12. 984; 13. 171;
14. 385; 15. 973; 16. 550; 17. 372; 18. 21;
19–20. Answers will vary.

Pages 51–52
A–B. Answers will vary. C. 20, 800, 300, 9,
70; D. 742, 247, Answers will vary. E. 98,
100, 102, 104; 120, 125, 130, 135; 353,
363, 373, 383; 182, 282, 382, 482; F. 284,
two hundred eighty-four, 200 + 80 + 4;
G. 1. >; 2. >; 3. =; 4. <; 5. <; 6. <; H. 87,
817, 868, 871; 504, 511, 514, 541; I. 76,
97, 89, 67; J. 65, 20, 35, 22; K. 82, 124,
100, 140; L. 66, 16, 39, 13; M–N. no, Check
students' work. O. 69, 127, 126, 115; P. 852,
822, Answers will vary.

Pages 53–54
1. ruler, meterstick, tape measure; 2. 2, 5;
3. centimeters, Answers will vary but should
include that centimeters are a smaller unit of
measure than inches. 4. Estimates will vary.
marker: 7 cm, crayon: 4 cm; 5. marker, 3 cm;
6. D; 7. Check students' work. 8. 11:10;
9. 93¢; 10. Students should add an X above
the 13. 2 action figures; 11. birds; 12. 26 days

Pages 55–56
1. tape measure, ruler, meter stick; 2. 3, 8;
3. Answers will vary but should include that
centimeters are a smaller unit of measure than
inches. 4. Estimates will vary. paper clip: 2 cm,
eraser: 3 cm; 5. paper clip, 1 cm; 6. B;
7. Check students' work. 8. 2:50; 9. 71¢;
10. 2 cm; 11. 15 people; 12. Students should
add half of a dot beside Rico. 45 students

Page 57
1. ruler; 2. tape measure; 3. ruler;
4. meterstick; 5. 8 inches; 6. 4 feet;
7. 15 centimeters; 8. 3 meters; 9. 6 yards;
10. 12 inches

Page 58
1. 2; 2. 3; 3. 5; 4. 5; 5. 6; 6. 4; 7. 12; 8. 9;
9. 1; 10. 7

© Carson-Dellosa • CD-104936

Answer Key

Page 61
1. 3 in., 8 cm; 2. 1 in., 3 cm; 3. 5 in., 12 cm;
4. 4 in., 9 cm; 5. 2 in., 5 cm; 6. Answers will
vary but should include that centimeters are
always greater because the unit is smaller.
7. greater than 3 cm, Answers will vary.

Page 62
Estimates will vary. 1. 6; 2.1; 3. 3; 4. 7; 5. 2;
6. 9; 7. 11; 8. 2; 9. 17; 10. 12

Page 63
1. ticket: 5, gum: 4, 1 cm; 2. feather: 4 in.,
leaf: 3, 1 in.; 3. nickel: 2 cm, candy: 11 cm,
9 cm

Page 64
1. 19 ft.; 2. 17 in.; 3. 91 in.; 4. 182 cm;
5. 16 cm; 6. 161 m

Page 65
1–3. Check students' work. 4. 12 ft.; 5. 7 m;
6. 19 yd.

Page 66
1. 12:35; 2. 3:50; 3. 7:25; 4–7. Check
students' work. 8. pm; 9. am; 10. early

Pages 67–68
A. J, 9:05; B. K, 12:30; C. L, 3:25; D. M,
4:10; E. N, 6:15; F. O, 1:40; G. P, 10:50;
H. Q, 8:35; I. R, 5:55

Pages 69–70
A. 41¢; B. 69¢; C. $1.61; D. 93¢; E. 96¢;
F. 80¢; G. 85¢; H. $1.15; I. $1.07; J. $1.38;
K. $1.64; L. $3.00; M. $3.13; N. $3.56

Page 71
1. 1, 5; 2. 1, 2, 10; 3. 1, 5, 25; 4. 2, 5, 10;
5. 4, 10, 20, 100; 6. $1.83; 7. $1.43;
8–9. Check students' work. 10. Answers
will vary.

Page 72
1. 84¢; 2. 57¢; 3. 77¢; 4. $1.93; 5. $1.08;
6. Sean, 5¢

Page 73
1. 10 in.; 2. 2 books; 3. 0; 4. 9 in.; 5. Check
students' work. 6. 13 caterpillars; 7. 13 cm;
8. Answers will vary.

Page 74
Check students' work. 1. 2 bookmarks;
2. 16 cm; 3. 2 bookmarks; 4. Check students'
work. 5. 11 bookmarks

Page 75
1. giraffe, 8 students; 2. 6 students;
3. 15 students; 4. 20 students, Answers will
vary but should include adding all of the
amounts. 5. tiger; Answers will vary but should
include that the tiger bar is taller.

Page 76
Check students' work. 1. brownie;
2. 1 customer; 3. 15 customers; 4. John;
5. 7 books; 6. 34 books

Page 77
1. Ashley; 2. 10 seeds; 3. Rachel, 2 more;
4. Zach; 5. 18 seeds; 6. no, Answers will vary
but should include reasoning about the key.

Page 78
1. Answers will vary depending on the key
chosen by each student. 2. T, F, T, T; 3. Answers
will vary. 4. 15 cans; 5. 175 items

Answer Key

Pages 79–80

A. ruler, tape measure, meterstick; B. 19 inches, 8 meters, 6 feet; C. 4, 2; D. 1, 3; E. 5, 2, Answers will vary but should refer to the sizes of the units. F. 3 cm; G. 19 ft.; H. 7, Answers will vary. I. Check students' work. J. 2:55, Check students' work. K. $1.01, $1.52; L. $4.01; M. Check students' work. N. Check students' work. O. 5 people; P. 17 days

Page 81

1. Check students' work. a shape with six sides and six angles; 2. 3, 4; 3. C; 4. Check students' work. 10; 5. Check students' work. fourths or quarters; 6. B

Page 82

1. Check students' work. a shape with four sides and four angles; 2. 5, 6; 3. A; 4. Check students' work. 8; 5. Check students' work. halves; 6. B

Page 85

1. pentagon, 5, 5; 2. trapezoid, 4, 4; 3. square, 4, 4; 4. hexagon, 6, 6; 5–8. Check students' work. 9. X: cube; They are 2-D shapes. 10. no, Answers will vary but should include that both shapes have five sides and five angles.

Page 86

1. Check students' work. 8; 2. Check students' work. 9; 3. Check students' work. halves; 4. Check students' work. fourths; 5. Check students' work. yes, Answers will vary but should include reasoning about the identical beginning shapes.

Pages 89–90

A. Check students' work. B. quadrilateral, 5, 6; C. Check students' work. D–E. Check students' work. Answers will vary. F–H. Check students' work. I. Check students' work. 12; J. 18, Check students' work. K–M. Check students' work. N. 1. thirds; 2. fourths; 3. fourths; 4. halves; O. yes, Answers will vary but should include reasoning about the identical beginning shapes. P. Check students' work.

Notes